M000200923

DATE DUE

Metro Litho
Oak Forest, IL 60452

C29

OTHER BESTSELLING BOOKS WRITTEN BY DEMPSEY J. TRAVIS

Harold: The People's Mayor
Real Estate is the Gold in Your Future
An Autobiography of Black Politics
An Autobiography of Black Jazz
An Autobiography of Black Chicago
Racism: American Style A Corporate Gift

I REFUSE TO

THE AUTOBIOGRAPHY OF
DEMPSEY J. TRAVIS

URBAN RESEARCH PRESS, INC.

DRUGS-RACISM-SELF-HATE

REX

Library of Congress Cataloging-in-Publication Data

Travis, Dempsey, 1920-
        I refuse to learn to fail / Dempsey J. Travis.
            p.   cm.
        Includes bibliographical references and index.
        ISBN 0-941484-12-2 :
            1. Travis, Dempsey, 1920-   . 2. Afro-Americans--Illinois-
Chicago--Biography. 3. Chicago (Ill.)--Biography. I. Title.
F548.9.N4T75   1992
977.3'110049607302--dc20
[B]   91-24222
                                                          CIP

Copyright 1992 Urban Research Press Inc.
840 East 87th Street, Chicago, Illinois 60619
All Rights Reserved
Printed in the United States of America

No part of this publication may be reproduced or transmitted in any
form or by any means, electronic or mechanical, including
photocopy, recording or any information storage and retrieval
system, without written permission from the publisher.

Photo Credits

Chicago Historical Society
Dollars & Sense Magazine
Library of Congress
Department of Defense
Urban Research Press

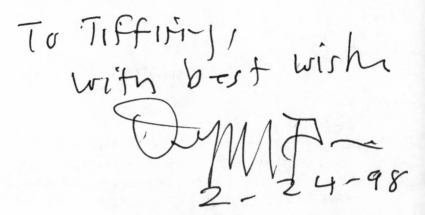

To Tiffiny,
with best wishes
[signature]
2-24-98

Dedication

This book is dedicated to Levar Lindsay Martin and Jamaal Ashon Martin, and to all African American young people who refuse to learn to fail.

May courage, commitment and community ignite the torch that will light their way to success.

Illustrations

Acknowledgments

I Refuse to Learn to Fail is a slice of my life story with a supporting cast of hundreds who individually held my hand at some point on a long and tough journey. To name all the members of the cast on a single page would be an impossible task. However, I want to take this opportunity to express gratitude to those kind souls, living and dead, who never let me walk alone.

Let me not forget to thank those who aided me in recording the events on this lap of the journey. First, my wife Moselynne, who denied herself the opportunity to wear a new formal gown to a black tie dinner dance where Tony Bennett was performing. She sacrificed the evening to enable me to finish this work on schedule.

Other members of my team who gave their all to meet the deadline were Ruby Davis, my Senior Researcher; Dorothy Parr Riesen, the editor; and Bessie Rahman, my Administrative Assistant and the youngest member of the staff.

Table of Contents

Dempsey J. Travis, 1938.

FOREWORD by Dr. Carl C. Bell, M.D., F.A.P.A.

In this book Dempsey J. Travis does an exemplary job of teaching by example. The principles highlighted by his examples and anecdotes are crucial to the survival of the African American community. The book illustrates attitudes and values we all need in order to do well in this country.

When Mr. Travis was "coming along" there were hostile forces pitted against the African American community's well-being, and those same forces are still present today but less obvious. Despite these negative influences such as poor health care, poor educational opportunities, poor housing, poor job opportunities, racial harassment, and more, people like Mr. Travis have done well and succeeded.

As an African American psychiatrist interested in the health and well-being of African Americans,

I have often wondered what it was that caused one of our brothers or sisters to stand tall in a hostile environment while others in the same circumstances fell by the wayside. This book illustrates the factors that I believe strengthened those of us who "made it." As a result, this is a book all African Americans should read if they want to succeed or to understand success.

Early in the book, it becomes clear that exemplary role models (i.e., specific persons who serve as examples for children to emulate and who teach specific attitudes, behaviors and skills necessary for survival) are crucial to achievement. Although all African American children have dreams of succeeding in life, African American children who have exemplary role models available to them are the ones who are most likely to achieve their goals. But children with a dream and no one to show them how to make their dreams come true become frustrated and angry. The nurturing aspects of a stable African American community are highlighted. The African American community was more stable during segregation, as there were all classes of African Americans living in close proximity to one another and they served as positive role models for each other's children.

Children had dreams and real people available

to supply a map for their dreams. When the civil rights desegregation movement got changed into an integration movement, some African Americans thought they needed to "whitewash" themselves and divest themselves of anything connected to their ethnic identity in order to fit into the American mainstream. This terrible error was made by some of us. We all should have maintained our ethnic identity and insisted on desegregation instead of integration, like all immigrants have done when coming to America. Studies have shown that African American children in integrated settings have lower self-esteem than children in desegregated settings.

In an integrated setting African American children must deny their heritage and be pro-white in order to fit in, while in a desegregated setting it is possible to be pro-African American and not be anti-white. There is nothing to prevent us from restabilizing our communities by not mistaking integration for desegregation, and returning to communities to restabilize them.

Many middle-class African Americans have acted to stabilize the African American community and continue to do so in 1992, but we need to understand the damage accepting integration has done. Mr. Travis illustrates how to give African American children the self-esteem they require to "make it."

Early in life, at age 5, his experiences almost produced a child whose self-image did not match their notion of what he should be like (i.e., his ego ideal). This was a crucial point in his development as self-esteem is the difference between how you think you are (self-image) and what you think you should be like (ego ideal). Fortunately, his mother, Mrs. Mittie Travis adjusted his self-image and ego ideal by letting him know that being Black was beautiful, and that he was her black velvet, which she described as the prettiest and most expensive material in the world, this experience firmly rooted young Dempsey in his own intrinsic value.

His stories about his first entrepreneurial activities as a child are revealing as they portray the importance of the Black community having a job base. We need a job base within our community so we can offer our own children those early childhood experiences that develop future business leaders. This book is a personal testimony that demonstrates the validity of the "locus of control" research on success. Although he was aware there were whites who were against him succeeding, Mr. Travis attributed his early academic failures to his lack of effort in going the extra mile at the high school level. He later said to himself "Although the white man is against me, the white man cannot keep me from learning and striving if I take responsibility for my education and future".

It is the development of this type of internal locus of control philosophy which has been shown to be a key factor for success. Mr. Travis' anecdotes clearly indicate that young African Americans should be taught to attribute their success to their ability and their failures to their lack of effort. If we continue to maintain an external locus of control philosophy, e.g., "The man won't let me get ahead," we will never try and try again until we succeed.

After his earlier years, when he was insulated and protected by his loving family, Mr. Travis clearly became exposed to the more overt hostile forces of racism. He illustrates the continuum of trauma African Americans suffer from microinsults to overt racially motivated violence. The trauma he experienced ranged from the microinsult of negative expectancy communications about his potential to learn to read, to more severe insults, like having to wait for a needed blood transfusion until the doctors could find some Negro Type A blood, to more overt violence of standing next to a friend who was shot to death by white U.S. military police for unjustified reasons. His "refusal to learn to fail" continued despite the violence and the lack of recognition for his excellence as an Army Post Exchange Manager. The glue that held his mental threads together was his sense of African and African American history that he had digested from listening to his mother, father and uncles and the pride he had in his people.

He understood the importance of initiative, in that he took Army correspondence courses in accounting, and also became a 50 words-per-minute, self-taught typist. These achievements were accomplished despite the institutional racism he was faced with in the military. He continued to strive and learn despite the institutional racism in the educational system. Mr. Travis realized he had responsibility for his mind and body when he asked, "How can I have a healthy body with a malnourished mind? A man is what he eats and a mind is what it reads." Finally, Mr. Travis learned the joy of learning and began to learn for learning's sake. Fortunately, unlike some of our brothers and sisters, Mr. Travis learned that education was not just "Whitey's thing," but it was also a "Black thing," a lesson all of our children need to learn.

Later, the book takes off into the more adult aspects of Mr. Travis' life and it becomes clear that there are no get-rich-quick schemes nor any short roads to success. He chronicles the early beginning of Harold Washington's and Gus Savage's careers and how it took them 32 years to reach their goals as U.S. congressmen. He provides an example of an African American middle-class tradition of providing service as an NAACP activist, but cautions us about an African American middle-class problem of "survivor guilt" in which upwardly mobile African Americans "make it" but feel so guilty that they give back so much they lose their gains.

Mr. Travis decries the other African American middle-class tradition of escapism, and underscores another African American survival strategy, i.e., to socialize upwardly mobile African Americans to give back to their people. The success of these strategies is evident in the commitment of African American physicians who graduate from African American medical schools such as Meharry Medical College in Nashville, Tennessee, toward serving the poor and underserved because they are professionally socialized to work within the African American community.

This is a good book written by a hard-hitting businessman that illustrates the concept that with a strong will, pride in being an African American and a good education, African American "street urchins" can succeed. I strongly recommend this book for book reports by young African American males and females. Dempsey Travis has supplied the world with another outstanding book that chronicles African American history, and, more importantly, he has provided African Americans a written personal odyssey on how to succeed.

Carl C. Bell
M.D., F.A.P.A.
Jan 5, 1992

Dr. Bell is the Executive Director of the Community Mental Health Council in Chicago, Illinois.

Introduction by Dr. Harvette Grey, Ph.D.

Dempsey J. Travis is a rare individual: a self-made multimillionaire African American man who gratefully acknowledges his family and community as the sources of his success.

Travis details the trials and tribulations of his memorable life in homage to his mother and father, wife, Moselynne, and maternal grandmother, Winnie Strickland, who endowed him with a positive, permanent identification with his race, and with the discipline and values that empowered him to obtain both personal and financial security.

This challenging autobiography is undergirded by the conviction that African American communities can be strong, viable, nurturing and vital; that African American heritage supersedes other issues, such as class; and that the nuclear family remains an important entity in the development of leadership within the African American community.

We are forced to ask what will happen to the youth of today who receive their only images of successful African American men and women from the mass media, a very effective weapon controlled by those outside of the African American community? Along with the rest of society, our young people are bombarded with erroneous depictions of impotence, drug pushers, prostitutes and other negative characterizations as the "normal" behavior of African Americans.

Dempsey Travis urges upper-class African Americans, to re-examine their exodus from their native communities. What is happening to these neighborhoods? What will happen to the potential leaders who will grow into men and women with little understanding of or regard for their less fortunate brothers and sisters?

This exploration of the dual roles that African Americans balance so delicately today is a continuation of the "dual consciousness" defined by W.E.B. DuBois more than 80 years ago. It contrasts the contemporary dilemma of the African American middle class who would forget their past as they fashion their future with the community's need for committed and understanding leadership within its physical and psychological boundaries.

Travis focuses on fighting back and beating the odds as the alternative to the demeaning insistence of the establishment notion that a people who have been denied boots should pick themselves up by their bootstraps. His response to that twisted logic of rugged individualism is the portrayal of an energetic, effective African American community in which all socioeconomic classes work together to produce an Afrocentric perspective.

This message is especially important at a time of national economic distress and the continued physical and psychological war on the African American family and community. The story of how Dempsey Travis refused to learn to fail is a clarion call to the Talented Tenth who have seized the prize: you cannot afford to allow failure to become the epitaph for the African American community.

Harvette Grey, Ph.D.
Clinical Psychologist
University of Illinois at Chicago

Mayor Harold Washington and Dempsey J. Travis on the stage of the Petrillo Band Shell at the 1984 Chicago Jazz Festival.

Prologue

The force that shoved me into writing "I Refuse to Learn to Fail" in the winter of my life was the recognition that some purpose might be served in sharing with others my more than seven decades of living, working and traveling around the world many times. In addition, the passing years have rendered an intense awareness that my duration on this planet is like a bubble going over Niagara Falls and that the sands in my hour glass of life are getting low.

My life experience dictates that Black people, traditionally the targets of racism in this country, cannot afford the added burden of class segregation. Yet more and more affluent African Americans are hastily separating themselves from their less fortunate brothers and sisters.

During the period when American restrictive housing covenants enforced segregation, upper- and middle-class Blacks and sports heroes such as Jessie Owens, Jackie Robinson, Joe Louis, Sugar Ray Robinson and Jack Johnson, the first black heavy weight champion, lived comfortably next door or down the street from people on welfare. That exotic mix of economic classes provided a unique community, a learning laboratory for the disadvantaged that has all but vanished. Our pursuit of creature comforts during the past three decades has diminished a large segment of African Americans' tolerance for those former neighbors who today are categorized by some as members of the underclass.

My folk heroes of yesteryears, unlike Topsy, did not grow up like wild weeds in a cotton patch. These strong willed Black men and women gloried in their roots and shared a common determination to refuse to learn to fail. Some of their contributions are told in this addition to my autobiographical series in the hope that their giant steps will not be lost like footprints in the sand but will lead us to understand how positive influences in our formative years can shape and motivate us to rise above the crowd.

Too many Black Americans whose impacts have extended beyond their own stomping grounds made their final exit from this planet without leaving a paper trail. The only records of their having come this way, unless they were famous musicians, entertainers or athletes, are usually buried in obituaries in local ethnic newspapers or nationally in Jet magazine.

Earl B. Dickerson is but one example of an African American whose success story deserves documentation. Earl witnessed the lynching of a relative in his home state of Mississippi when he was an adolescent. His widowed mother, a washerwoman, bundled up her young son and sent him to Chicago, where she hoped he might have a better chance to overcome the traumatic experience and make something of himself.

Dickerson more than fulfilled his mother's ambitions for him and grew up to excel in the fields of law and business. The brilliant attorney became chairman of the board and president of the Supreme Life Insurance Co. More importantly, he was a fearless champion of civil rights, an ally of W.E.B. DuBois, Paul Robeson and other stalwarts of the era.

Other influential business and civic leaders of my generation included George S. Harris, president of the National Association of Real Estate Brokers for many years and president of the Chicago Metropolitan Mutual Assurance Co., and Dr. Theodore K. Lawless, an internationally renowned dermatologist and philanthropist who was one of the founders of Service Federal Savings and Loan

Association, now known as Illinois Service Federal Savings and Loan Association.

Dickerson, Harris and Lawless were prominent in national Black life for more than four decades, and their names were household words throughout Black, Brown and Beige America. A recommendation from any of them could open doors to careers in business and politics and to civic and social opportunities that might otherwise have remained closed. Dickerson, one of my role models, opened doors for John H. Johnson, publisher of Ebony and Jet magazines; Harris opened many doors for me; Lawless opened doors for Dr. Harold W. Thatcher and many other physicians.

Black heroes of the first half of this century are generally unknown to people of color under 60 years of age. Yet those leaders typify the citizens Dr. W.E.B. DuBois referred to in 1903 when he said, "The Negro Race, like all races, is going to be saved by its exceptional people...The Talented Tenth." Much of the blame for their exclusion from American textbooks, and Black history books in particular, rests with Black writers and scholars but more heavily on the shoulders of white publishers in that they are the gate keepers of the mind.

As a writer and publisher I recognize that short memories are a fact of life. My early awareness of the potential for greatness of my lifelong friend Harold Washington led me to record some of his

Theodore K. Lawless
Dec. 6, 1892 - May 1, 1974

Earl B. Dickerson
June 22, 1891 - Aug. 31, 1986

W.E.B. DuBois
Feb. 23, 1868 - Sept. 27, 1963

George S. Harris
Aug. 8, 1898 - Sept. 8, 1980

accomplishments in the seven books I have written between 1980 and 1992. One of which was "Harold: The People's Mayor," published by Urban Research Press in January 1989, 14 months after his death.

Washington authorized me to write his biography only after deciding that he might not have time to write the story himself. Our taping sessions, conducted over a period of four years beginning in May 1983, took place in a variety of settings in the United States and overseas.

During our conversations it became clear that Harold's idol was not to be found among the celebrated political, entertainment and sports figures he had known. His chief role model was his father, Attorney Roy Washington, Sr. Their home was visited by a host of prominent Black Chicago leaders and Mr. Washington made sure that their lessons on success were not lost on his children.

Young Harold was particularly impressed with Oscar DePriest, a lifelong Republican and Chicago's first Black alderman and congressman; Arthur W. Mitchell, the first Black Democrat to be elected to Congress from Chicago; and William L. Dawson "the man", who served as U.S. Representative from the 1st Congressional District for 27 years.

Washington realized that members of later generations were not automatic heirs to the nurturing of intellectual curiosity and idealism that permeated his childhood, and therefore early in his career he eagerly accepted invitations to speak and teach at colleges and schools in the Chicago metropolitan area. His enthusiasm for meeting with and encouraging young people continued as he gained national prominence and addressed student bodies around the country to the end of his life.

Harold's convictions about the presence of strong role models in the community were also evident in his personal life. He lived in the Third Ward for 60 of his 65 years. He was comfortable in every milieu, from shooting pool in the heart of a public housing development to conversing with the pope or a president.

The class stratification that propels Buppies to flee their mother wards for the suburbs was alien to Harold's nature. His goal throughout his political career was to enfold people from all walks of life into a sense of real community. One of the most appropriate tributes to "The People's Mayor" who was a cafeteria reader, is the Harold Washington Library Center in Chicago, which became the largest public library in the nation when it opened on October 7, 1991. An inscription near the entrance of this $150 million facility begins with a quote from Mayor Washington:

"Chicago...has brought together Black and White, Asian and Hispanics, male and female, the young, the old...."

This is his legacy for all Americans.

Why can't we, too, refuse to learn to fail?

Dempsey J. Travis
January 5, 1992

In 1922, when I was two years old, with my mother, Mrs. Mittie Travis.

CHAPTER

Beautiful Black Velvet

When I was 5 years old, we were the first African-Americans to move into a 24-flat building at 3609 S. Cottage Grove Ave. in Chicago, Ill.

Many of the pre-teenage white boys who lived there made a game of scaring the happiness out of me almost every day. Even their appearance intimidated me: I had never been around anyone with ghostly, chalklike skin and yellow, corn-silk hair. To my young eyes, they resembled uncaged felines as they sat at the top of the steep staircase with their pale blue, green, gray and hazel eyes glistening in the dimly lit hallway in front of our apartment door.

Some days they even hissed like wild tom

cats; sometimes they would bark like mad dogs in August. No matter what sounds they made, they scared me more than the rumbling of earthshaking thunder in a rainstorm or the shrill scream of the siren on a speeding hook-and-ladder fire truck.

One day one of those boys called me a "Black son of a bitch." Those strange words flooded through his twisted lips and protruding gapped teeth. The harshness of his voice frightened me so that I ran to my mother, who was in our apartment, and repeated what he said.

To my surprise, mother did not show anger, she simply smiled.

"Have you ever seen black velvet?" she asked, stroking the back of my head with her left hand while reaching with her right hand into her dresser drawer. She gently pulled out a beautiful black velvet jacket for me to examine.

I touched it carefully and observed, "It's soft and pretty." Mother slipped her left arm around my shoulders. "This is the best and most expensive material in the world," she said.

"It is?"

"You are my black velvet," she answered tenderly.

That simple exchange provided me with the wisdom of relating to my Blackness in a very positive way. Since that incident, I have refused to learn to fail in spite of the racial barriers and other obstacles that have been thrown in my path as I climbed the ladders of life. Both my mother and father taught me that internalizing negative and grossly inaccurate self-images about our Blackness ensures failure, no matter what paths we choose to follow.

Travis, the five year old entrepreneur reluctantly poses for a photo.

2

CHAPTER

My First Business Ventures

1925 was a silver year for me; the year I decided to enter the business world at age 5. The idea of being a boy in business was inspired by the sight of a brand-new red tricycle, which was owned by Charles Murray Jr., an African-American lad my age. His father, Charles Murray Sr., drove a 1925 pale green Buick with side mount tires on both front fenders. The car was new, just like the tricycle.

Charles senior manufactured and distributed hair pomade out of five storefronts across the street from where we lived. Murray's Hair Pomade was to African-Americans in the 1920s and '30s what Fashion Fair and Soft Sheen are today.

I did not know if my father would ever own

a new Buick, but I knew that one day I would use Murray's Hair Pomade, and I did. I tried to look like the handsome man pictured on the pomade's orange tin container.

A few weeks after I first saw young Charles and his tricycle, a man opened a barbershop in a storefront in our neighborhood. I asked him if he needed a young barber. He replied, "No, but I need someone to pass out my business cards," and said he would pay me 50 cents. I accepted his offer without telling my parents and started work immediately.

I was not satisfied with simply distributing the barber's cards in front of his shop as he had instructed me; I had to cover both sides of Cottage Grove which was a busy thoroughfare. While running across the street to give a man a card, I spied a streetcar, "Big Red," headed straight at me. I dodged it just in time—just in time to be hit by a Black open-top Model T Ford coming up on my blind side.

When I woke up, I was in Provident Hospital at 36th and Dearborn Avenue. My mother and a man dressed in a white smock were standing at the foot of the bed.

My mother was crying and wringing her hands and asking, "Is he going to be all right?"

"He doesn't seem to be too badly injured," the doctor assured her. "All he seems to have suffered is a fractured left leg."

Mom began to smile a little, but didn't seem convinced until she leaned over the bed and tickled the bottom of my right foot. I giggled and her broad smile lit up the room. She turned to the doctor and said, "Yes, he's going to be all right."

My first business venture ended with me colliding with a car and my sponsor bringing me a basket full of apples, oranges and pears, and an extra dollar for service rendered beyond the call of duty.

My next entrepreneurial excursion began several months later, three weeks before Thanksgiving. The Sunday comic strips carried an advertisement that offered a toy electric train to any boy or girl who could sell 200 miniature, multicolored bottles of perfume.

My mother mailed the newspaper coupon to the company and I received a shipment of perfume on December 1. I was determined to sell enough to win an electric train for Christmas.

My sales efforts were riddled with problems. Almost everyone I approached sniffed from a bottle of the perfume and frowned. However, for reasons I did not understand at the time, some people smiled at me, handed me 10 cents, and told me to keep the perfume. I was unable to sell enough bottles to be awarded the train.

Disappointed, but not downhearted, I took on the task of selling the <u>Chicago Defender</u> weekly

"Young Dempsey was successful as a newsboy."

newspaper. During those days, paperboys had to pay for their papers in advance. I purchased the newspapers for 6 cents each and sold them for a dime. I usually sold at least 10 Defenders every Friday afternoon on the southwest corner of 35th and Cottage Grove, across the street from Walgreen, the second in the chain that currently boasts more than 1,000 stores. My weekly profit of 40 cents enabled me to go to the theater every Saturday and Sunday afternoon and have enough change left to buy candy and peanuts. I continued this successful operation until I was 9 years old.

In 1929, the year of the Great Depression, I got a job working out of a newspaper branch office at 4711 S. Langley as a delivery boy for the Chicago American, a white-owned afternoon newspaper. I was selected over several other boys because of my experience with the Chicago Defender. Ernest Bush, an acting assistant branch manager who years later became a successful general contractor in Chicago, taught me how to roll and throw newspapers.

As a newsboy, I learned a great deal about dealing with the public and handling money. I enjoyed the feeling of independence that comes with working unsupervised. The best part of the job was the joy of having extra money to buy pies and cakes from the grocery stores and bakeries as I walked along my paper route.

Louis Travis, father of Dempsey J. Travis, at the piano in their home at 3609 S. Cottage Grove Ave. in January, 1926.

3

CHAPTER

The Music Man

In 1925, my father gave our family a wonderful Christmas gift: an upright player piano, which he purchased on an installment plan. The piano made music two ways: you could play its 88 black and white keys manually or you could insert a perforated paper roll and by see sawing the piano pedals with your feet, activate the keys to jump up and down and spill out such popular tunes as "I'm Looking at the World Through Rose Colored Glasses," "Am I Blue?," "Rose of the Rio Grande," "That Old Gang of Mine," and "Sweethearts on

Parade." My dad and I enjoyed taking turns at pumping the piano, although my feet could barely reach the pedals when I sat on the piano stool.

My father played skillfully without learning to read music, but he was determined that his son would learn to be a music-reading pianist. Dad had a torrid relationship with boogie-woogie blues tones, but felt comfortable about teaching them to me as long as I took "real" lessons.

A family friend told my father that I should begin piano lessons by using the Matthews Music Primer. Mother contacted Elmer Simpson, a gifted college-trained musician who was the music director for many years at Grant Memorial A.M.E. Church. Mr. Simpson came to our house once a week to give me a half-hour lesson for 50 cents plus 14 cents for his round-trip streetcar fare. My first formal lesson was held seven weeks before my sixth birthday on February 25, 1926.

Within a few weeks of practice, Mr. Simpson had prepared me to play "Violets Blue" in a children's musical recital held at the West Point Baptist Church, which is still located on the northwest corner of 36th and Cottage Grove. My parents had been very pleased with my ability to play a simple melodic scale with some rapidity, and Dad didn't hesitate to voice his delusions about his son's future. His first words after we left the church were, "Earl 'Fatha' Hines look out, 'cause my boy is coming!"

My mother said, "Sweetheart, you're crazy!"

Dad just looked at her with a smile, and tightened his grip on my hand as we walked home.

During those days I came alive only after school, when I practiced and fooled around on the piano. By the time I reached the sixth grade at Francis C. Willard Elementary School, I was a really good player, but not as good as my classmates Dorothy Donegan, John Young, Willie Webb, and Robert Anderson. Both Webb and Anderson became nationally famous musicians and gospel singers.

This photograph of Travis' grade 7B class at the Willard Elementary School was taken in 1932. Dempsey Travis is pictured in the top row, second from the right. Also pictured are the late Jessie Miller, famous band leader and trumpet player (top row, 1st from the left), and Robert Anderson, gospel pianist and singer (top row, 3rd from the right).

I sometimes practiced with Herbert Moore, a clarinet player who also attended Willard Elementary. We played tunes like "Lazy Bones" and "When

Your Hair Has Turned to Silver," as well as Duke Ellington's "Sophisticated Lady."

Sophisticated is what we thought we were. I was almost certain I would be the next Duke Ellington. Herbert and I played a duet at Willard School when we were 11 years old. My first band was formed when we added a guitar player, Jessie Miller, to our combo. Miller later became an excellent trumpet player and popular band leader at Club Delisa in Chicago. For the next several years, it seemed I was always organizing musicians for some event.

Earl Hines and his orchestra, 1941. Left to right: (front) Earl Hines, Franz Jackson, Scoops Carry, Willie Randall, Leroy Harris, Jimmy Mundy; (middle) Ed Fant, George Hunt, Joe McLewis; (back) George Dixon, Tommy Nixon, Benny Harris.

My father, who usually retired quite early in the evening, insisted that I go to bed before he did. I would turn out the light, crawl into bed and pull a sheet over my head until I heard him snoring. Then I'd sneak back into the living room, turn on the radio with the volume at a whisper and listen to great Black bands from the Cotton Club in the Harlem section of New York City and from the Grand Terrace on the South Side of Chicago. Sitting there in the

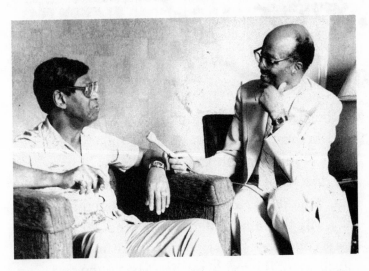

Dempsey J. Travis, right, interviewing Earl Hines, his piano mentor in the Summer of 1983.

dark, straining to hear the music, I became intoxicated by the piano magic of both Duke Ellington and Earl "Fatha" Hines and was confident that one day I, too, would be a star on the radio.

Radio wasn't my only entree to great music.

2 ← FAMOUS ORCHESTRAS → 2
WARWICK HALL
EVERY THURSDAY NITE

Presenting

Chicago's New Young Maestro
JACK TRAVIS & HIS ORCHESTRA
THURSDAY, NITE MARCH 31ST

GENERAL ADMISSION 25¢

LADIES 10¢ Before 9:30 p. m. ·+· CHECKING FREE

The Jack Travis Orchestra played for dances at the Warwick Hall at 543 East 47th Street.

Mother took me downtown every time a famous Black orchestra—like those led by Louis Armstrong, Duke Ellington, Cab Calloway, Jimmy Lunceford and dozens of others—played at the Oriental, Chicago, State-Lake, and Palace theaters in the Loop.

By the time I entered high school, I was even more confident that I would make a living as a musician for the rest of my life. My combo had been playing for fun for more than two years and from time to time we would actually get a job that paid $2 per man per night. Our wages were not bad in the days when most Blacks earned less than $25 per week.

Capt. Walter Dyett, the renowned bandleader at DuSable High School, called me "the little big shot" and refused to let me play in the Booster Band until my junior year because I was too cocky. I was 15 years old at the time and, in spite of my bragging, I knew I had a lot to learn. Dyett didn't mind telling me so, either. But I really wanted to play with a good group, and when Dyett wouldn't let me play in his, I organized my own big band. At age 16, I became the youngest card-carrying orchestra leader in the Local 208 Musicians Union. Our group didn't get any jobs immediately, but we rehearsed a lot.

One morning I saw an ad in the <u>Chicago Tribune</u>:

> **WANTED**
> **FOUR PIECE COMBO**
> To play at Dime-a-Dance Hall
> 335 S. Wabash
> Apply in person

I was excited about the gig. I had to look just right. I dressed up in my best Sunday suit and combed my hair. Thank God I used Murray's Pomade and wore a stocking cap to bed the night before.

I raced downtown and located the office of the dance hall. The manager looked up from some papers, blew a couple of smoke rings from his big cigar in my face, and asked, "What do you want? Are you applying for the washroom porter job?"

"No. I am a bandleader," I replied with pride.

I had practiced what I was going to say during my ride on the elevated train from the South Side. The words came out of my mouth a mile a minute.

"I've got one of the hottest four-piece bands in town. We're well organized, well-disciplined, and we can really do the job you want done." My heart was beating so loudly I could hardly hear what I was saying.

He looked at me for a moment. My heart stood still. I was sure he was going to say I was too young. He took another puff on his cigar.

"What's the name of your band?" he asked.

" Jack Travis and his Orchestra", I retorted.

"Can you have your band here at 2 o'clock tomorrow afternoon for an audition?" he asked. "I want to hear them."

"You bet I can," I replied.

I was so on fire that I turned around and ran out the door and down the stairs without even saying goodbye. I wanted to tell the world I was a professional musician.

I also wanted to contact the other members of my band, and that was a problem. It was already dusk and two of the fellows did not have telephones. I ran all over the neighborhood and by 9:30 p.m., had found all three. It was fortunate that we had practiced so much, because we didn't have time for a rehearsal. The two guys with day jobs had to arrange for half a day off.

We had agreed to meet across from the dance hall at 1:30 the next day to make sure we wouldn't be late. I was there by 1 o'clock. Nick Cooper, the trumpet player; Elliott Lane, the alto sax man; and Chauncy Murdock, the drummer, were there by 1:15. We walked around the block for 40 minutes, instruments and all, so we wouldn't be too early. We didn't want to seem too eager—after all, we were supposed to be cool and professional.

And we were. We really laid it on that guy with the cigar. I didn't know we could play that well.

And that was only the beginning. We expanded the band to 12 men and played the Savoy Ballroom, the Warwick Hall, the Forum Hall and Bacon's Casino, playing more jobs than the members of Dyett's Booster Band.

We worked almost every weekend, but those gigs didn't come out of thin air. I had to go out and sell the package to people who could use combos and large orchestras, and became pretty good at it.

My father had found an effective way of punishing me when I did not come directly home after we finished our sets. He would stop me from playing music, and that was painful, because I loved the work. In early years, he made me quit a lucrative paper route the first time I was caught smoking. The positive approach to work he instilled has guided me successfully through several changes in vocations during the past seven decades.

Left: Chauncey Willard, the five-foot-tall principal of DuSable High School, had a voice of authority that clapped like thunder. He had the full respect of both the faculty and the student body. Right: Annabel C. Prescott, assistant principal and daughter of the late Bishop Archibald C. Carey, Sr. and the sister of the late Judge Archibald Carey, Jr.

Jean Baptist DuSable High School at 4934 S. Wabash Ave

4

CHAPTER

School Days

My formal education began at a private kinder-garten. At home, my parents proudly encouraged me to count to 100, recite the alphabet and quote simple poems and rhymes for their friends. I was pleased with myself and with school.

Suddenly my whole world changed.

Father became ill and we could no longer afford the tuition for private school, so I was sent to Doolittle Elementary, one block north of our home on 35th Street. With the exception of the teachers, the population of the first public school I attended was

African-American.

In first grade my teacher was Florence Green, a white woman. For reasons I have never fathomed, I did not like Ms. Green and she did not like me. I felt that the teacher and the Doolittle School were bad dreams that would go away in the mornings like any other nightmares. They didn't. I started playing hooky from school at the beginning of my third week.

To my 6-year-old mind, it seemed I stayed away from school for months, although I spent only a few days throwing rocks, kicking tin cans, bottles, and other junk in the alleys while my parents thought I was attending class.

One rainy morning about 10:30, a truant officer spotted me sitting on the stoop of an apartment building, took me by the hand and led me back to Doolittle. I was glad I had been caught and happier still when Ms. Green refused to accept me back in her class. At her request, I was transferred to the room of an African-American teacher. I had no problem with her. Although, I cannot recall her name, I vividly recall her earth-brown, oval smiling face.

We moved to 4826 S. Evans Ave. in 1931. I transferred to Willard Elementary School and graduated from there in January 1935.

The next month, I enrolled as a freshman at the new Wendell Phillips High School located at 4934 S. Wabash, the first high school built for Blacks in the Black community in Chicago. The place was so new that decorators were busy painting the corridor walls the day the school opened its doors for business. I was one of 1,300 freshmen out of a total enrollment of 3,548 boys and girls who attended classes in the building that was designed to accommodate 2,500 students. The students were African-American except for one white girl named Jewell, who was the daughter of a janitor employed at a large neighborhood apartment building. She was transferred out in the middle of my first semester.

The large enrollment had been caused by an early morning fire at the old Wendell Phillips High School in January 1935. Authorities closed down that facility and transferred the office staff, faculty, records, trophies, students and traditions into a new $3 million high school that was critically short of books, supplies and space. The name of the school, which was not scheduled to open until September 1935, was changed to Jean Baptiste Pointe DuSable in May 1936. John H. Johnson, chairman of the board of Johnson Publishing Company Inc., Fashion Fair Cosmetics, radio station WJPC-AM, and other enterprises, was the president of the graduating class that year.

DuSable High School classmates of Travis included such personalities as Nat "King" Cole (top left); John H. Johnson (top right) as he appears today and a youthful rendering of the businessman in 1936; Dorothy Donegan (bottom left), the famous piano artist; Redd Foxx (John Elroy Sanford) (bottom center), the popular comedian squatting playing the wash tub, and Savannah Strong (bottom right), brilliant song stylist of the 1940s.

5

CHAPTER

Job Hunting in the Real World

DuSable High School nurtured many talents, including Mayor Harold Washington, Judge William Cousins, Dr. Allen Wright, Dr. Alice Blair and comic Redd Foxx, whose real name was John Elroy Sanford. Nat "King" Cole was in my Spanish class. He and other great musical talents like pianists Dorothy Donegan, John Young, Martha Davis; singer Johnny Hartmann; and Johnny Griffin, master tenor saxophone player, left the assembly hall of the high school and achieved international stardom. The sparkplug that ignited them all was the legendary Capt. Dyett.

In the weeks before our graduation in June of 1939, DuSable seniors talked a lot about the dismal job picture for African Americans. We knew well enough that for us there were few "clean" jobs, other than clerking at the post office or working as railroad Pullman porters. There were no Black bus drivers, no Black streetcar operators or conductors and no Black motormen on elevated trains. There were no Blacks working in responsible positions in the neighborhood banks or in the ghetto branches of major life insurance companies or national retail chains. Blacks had no hope of being hired as cashiers or of working behind the lunch counter in the Walgreen drugstores in our own communities.

Racism was inescapable. We could not ignore the "For Whites Only" ads in the daily newspapers or on the notices posted on plant gates after World War II spurred more industrial employment. The job situation was so bad that some of my schoolmates deliberately failed courses in order not to graduate and be forced to join that weary army of Blacks who went from factory gate to factory gate every day in search of jobs that did not exist for them.

I shook my head in despair with the others, but in my heart I somehow knew it was going to turn out differently for me. Hadn't I been working for

years in music? Didn't I have a skill to sell?

Yet, by 1939 even jobs for Black musicians were drying up. The craze for "Black jazz" had turned to a craze for "white swing" played by the orchestras of Benny Goodman, Artie Shaw, and the Jimmy and Tommy Dorsey aggregation, who made thousands of dollars per week. At the same time, talented Black musicians who were employed through President Franklin D. Roosevelt's Federal Arts Project practiced their craft in public parks and community halls and tried to make ends meet on an average salary of $55 a month.

But what did that matter to me, when all I needed was just one job?

My father stared solemnly at me whenever I boasted about avoiding becoming an unemployment statistic. He knew it was time for me to face reality on my own. By September, I had worn the soles off several pairs of shoes, trudging from one club to another in search of full-time work as a musician. Dad grew more and more silent as I recounted my many disappointments.

Then, on the Tuesday morning after Labor Day, Dad came into my room and awakened me.

"Boy, if you're going to get a job, you have to be the first one in line at the employment office," he said.

"What?"

"Get up," he ordered. He watched as I stumbled out of bed and reached for my clothes. "This is how it's going to be," he said. "You can't drive your car until you find a job. I'm going to give you 14 cents for streetcar fare every day, and 50 cents for lunch money. You understand?"

"Yes, sir," I said.

"Don't spend the lunch money unless you get a job."

"No, sir," I nodded.

My father had a cousin who worked at the Armour soap works at 31st and Bensen and a friend employed by a starch factory in the 2900 block on Archer Avenue. The businesses were three blocks apart, so Dad decided that I would visit both places on this first day of hunting for daytime employment in the real world.

I walked from our third-floor apartment at 5428 S. Indiana Ave. to 51st to catch the streetcar and rode north to 31st, where I transferred to a west-bound trolley. The other riders were loud-talking Blacks, bragging about how they had spent Labor Day. Some wore blue denim overalls, and a few wore their Sunday best. When we reached Wentworth, oddly dressed white folks who spoke with foreign accents and smelled of garlic boarded the trolley. In the several blocks between Wentworth and Halsted, "Big Red" collected an overflow of clientele, causing five or six men and women to stand on the rear steps of the trolley and hold the door's center bar and side handles for support.

The air around the Armour soap plant stank, but it was not as overwhelming as the foul odor that drifted north from the stockyards. Following my father's instructions, I bypassed Armour and walked over the South branch of the Chicago River to the starch factory, where I waited alone outside the main entrance. After about an hour, a tall blond man in white overalls came to the door. With a snotty expression on his face, he said, "Boy, we ain't hiring today!"

Before I could say, "What about tomorrow?," he had disappeared into the bowels of the factory. Spiritually I felt lower than the chilling September temperature. I recrossed the bridge with the wind at my back and headed for the Armour and Company employment office which was housed in a one-story 19th century red-faced brick building.

An elderly white man about 55 years old sat at a desk behind a 3-foot wooden railing. Facing him were 10 rows of hardwood benches filled with men— Black, brown, and white, young and old. Some sat erect with their eyes focused on the old man at the desk. I felt a kinship with them. They appeared to be new in the job market, too. The oldtimers sat slumped, and alternately glanced hopelessly at the floor, the

Janitors picketing the Mid-City Realty to increase their weekly wages from $8.00 to $10.00 per week. Thus, enabling them to buy food other than corn meal and beans to feed their families.

walls and the ceiling, but seldom casting an eye at the middle-aged labor recruiter.

Occasionally the phone would ring and everyone would look up. The gray haired, wrinkled pruned face old man at the desk would beckon one or two of the bench warmers to come forward. They were usually sent directly to work without the benefit of work clothes or rubber boots. I learned that some of these jobs would last only a half-day or perhaps as long as a week, if they were lucky.

I repeated my trips to the starch factory and the soap works for 69 consecutive days, excluding Sundays. Job hunting was one of the coldest, loneliest and most dehumanizing experiences of my life. Each day ended as it started, except that the soles of my shoes and the seat of my pants became thinner.

My father correctly decided my only chance was to buy a job and directed me to the Factory Employment Agency located on East Van Buren between Wabash and State. For $10, I got a job as a porter for the Apex Box Company at 2509 W. Cermak Rd. The job paid 28 cents per hour, or $11.20 per week.

Art Blancher was the only other African American worker at Apex. He was a freight elevator operator and order filler who had a coffee-brown complexion and a quick smile that was a perfect window for his straight pearly teeth. Art was respected by the bosses and other employees because of his businesslike no-nonsense attitude. The other employees were either Italian or Polish women; most of them were Polish. The plant owners were German Jews.

With Art's assistance, I made the mental adjustments necessary to perform my portering duties with dispatch. My tasks included cleaning and mopping four two-stall washrooms and sweeping the plant floors throughout the day. After a month on the job, I was commended by my supervisors and by the vice president of the company for performing my chores with pride and enthusiasm.

My father had taught me early in life not to accept money for any assignment that I did not intend to do well. As a laborer at Wilson & Co., Dad pulled hams out of pickled-filled vats in a temperature of 30 degrees, but he made his work sound important and exciting.

"I pulled two more vats of hams today than Polish Joe and Mexican Frank, who was not even in the running," he would sometimes say.

My father talked about his job wih the excitement of describing a world class sports event.

Drawing a weekly paycheck made me feel secure enough to make a regular contribution to the family treasurer, Mother. She balanced the housing and food budget, deposited 25 percent of the combined salaries in a joint savings account, and was the sole judge of how much Dad and I would be permitted to spend foolishly on the weekends. We both respected her ability to manage our incomes. She was so debt-conscious that she felt the monthly rent was delinquent if it was not paid seven days before it was due.

My days at Apex went without conflict until March 9, 1940.

Zinky Cohn, the business agent for Local 208, the Black musicians' union, had asked me to put together a seven-piece band for a job at a West Side dance hall. I was overjoyed about the opportunity and the fact that the three-hour gig paid $6 to each sideman and $10 to me as the bandleader. That sum almost doubled my income that week.

All was well that evening until the band started playing "Sunny Side of the Street" and I looked down from the bandstand and saw four white girls from the box company smiling and waving. I practically fell off the piano bench, because I knew that Travis the porter could never explain Jack Travis the bandleader to those "ofays." Blacks, of course, understood the dual role we had to play in the American scheme of things, but somehow I couldn't bear the idea of explaining that dilemma to whites, since they created the problem.

I could accept my menial job as a porter as long as I kept it separated from my "real" life as a musician. But this sudden collision of my two worlds left me feeling confused and ashamed.

I did not return to Apex. Surrendering that job was the price I paid for my pride and principle. In retrospect, the price seems small, even though it meant walking the streets with 200,000 other jobless Chicagoans. It took only two days for me to decide I would use the $10 I made on the music gig to buy another job.

I have always known that your job is important. The information most people want to know about you after they learn your name is what kind of work you do. Unfortunately, most people equate the worth of an individual with their job titles and salaries.

The USS Arizona was one of the more seriously damaged United States ships at Pearl Harbor on December 7, 1941. Many of the more than 2,000 officers and enlisted men killed at Pearl were buried alive in ships like the

6

CHAPTER

An Invitation to the Killing Field

Nine months to the day following the bombing of Pearl Harbor on December 7, 1941, my mother told me when I arrived home from work that hot August afternoon, that she had placed a letter on my night table.

"Who would be writing me a letter?" I asked.

"Since I didn't open it, I would suggest that you read it and see," she replied.

I opened the envelope and the first word I saw in bold type was "GREETINGS." The letter continued, "You are hereby notified that you have been selected for training and service in the United States Armed Forces. Your local board will furnish transportation to an induction center....There you will be examined, and, if accepted...you will be inducted into the U.S. Army or Naval forces. Willful failure to report subjects the violator to a fine and imprisonment."

As I sat on the bed staring at the notice, mother called from the kitchen, "Who was the letter from?"

"The draft board," I said.

"The who?" she replied.

"The Army, Mama," I yelled.

Mother rushed into the bedroom and snatched the letter from my hand. She read it twice and repeated in prayerful tones, "I know Uncle Sam is not going to take my only child. I know Uncle Sam is not going to take my only child."

"Mama, 'the man' wants some cannon fodder and he ain't making no exceptions," I wailed.

My little world came to an abrupt end when I reported to the induction center and passed the physical examination. They ordered me to report back to my draft board which was located at 55th and Michigan Avenue Sept. 9, 1942, to be transported to the Illinois Central Railroad Station, where I would board a train for Fort Custer in Battle Creek, Mich.

I spent the last 10 days before leaving for the Army partying. The best times consisted of "joint hopping" from the Keyhole Lounge at 39th and South Parkway (King Drive) to the Red Moon Lounge on east 61st Street. Sometimes we would cover as many as 15 clubs in one evening. On my last night as a civilian, Claude Jenkins gave a party in my honor at his mother's home at 59th and Prairie. He had invited about 20 fellows including Charlie Murray Jr., the tricycle boy; Joe Simmons; Everett "Jelly" Martin; and Milton Turner. The party broke up about 4 a.m. I was in such bad shape that some of my friends had to walk me home.

I had been in bed only an hour when Dad woke me up to wish me good luck and ask me to write. An hour later, Mother shook my bed and said, "It's time for you to get up and go to the draft board."

She was putting up a brave front. I didn't realize it immediately, but my mother's face looked as if she had been crying all night. She had packed a big suitcase for me. I looked at her and said, "All I need, Ma, according to the instructions, are a few personal items such as a toothbrush, a comb and a change of underclothes."

She responded tearfully, "You have got to have two pairs of pajamas." and reluctantly un-packed the suitcase, lifting each piece as gingerly as she would have lifted a baby. "Why do they have to take my only child? Why do they have to take my only child?," she cried. Then she began to shake and scream: "Why Lord? Why are they taking my only child?"

I said, "Mother, I don't know," and then I began to cry. Without saying goodbye, I dashed out of the kitchen door and down the back stairs, sob-bing loudly: "Mama! I don't want to go! Mama! I don't want to go!"

At 8 a.m. sharp, the draftee bus was loaded and ready to go—with or without me. The 35-minute ride from Garfield Boulevard and Michigan to the Illinois Central train station at 12th and Michigan passed quickly because my mind was absorbed in the past.

It was not until I boarded the train an hour later with a group of about 100 other Black draftees that I began to feel like a bull among a herd of stockyard cattle being led to slaughter by a belled goat. (The stockyards used trained goats to lead cattle to the slaughter house. A single goat would lead several thousand cows and bulls to their deaths daily.)

The herd instinct helped deliver the cattle to the killing floor. What was driving me? Was it loyalty? Was it fear? Was it propaganda? Was it the opportunity for a Black man to fry and prove again that he was a first-class American?

"Battle Creek! Battle Creek!" yelled the conductor.

"Follow me," shouted our group leader as he waved his arms toward the front of the train. After we debarked, we were instructed to jump into the Army trucks that were lined up to take us into Fort Custer.

Travis' first military home was Fort Custer in Michigan. Pictured here are recruits standing in formation in front of their barracks at this installation named for the famed Indian fighter.

Within 20 minutes, we had reached the company area of the 1609th Service Unit. The "old" soldiers (three days in service) were laughing and shouting, "Shorty got your gal and gone" from the balcony and windows of the double-decked barracks that would be my home for the next four years.

We were left standing in the streets for about 10 minutes before a tall, slim, shifty-eyed man came out of the barracks and for several minutes looked at us as though we were transparent.

"I am 1st Sgt. Hammond," he said. "We are going to process you through this reception center within three or four days and then you will be shipped to another camp for your basic training."

At this point, the sergeant was distracted by a draftee who was talking. "What's your name soldier?" he demanded.

"John Rose," the recruit replied.

Hammond wrote his name down and said, "Soldier, if I catch you with your big trap open again, I am going to make you think hell is paradise compared to this place." He gave Rose a monster stare, turned and walked back to the center column where he announced that Buck Sgt. Willie Moore would be in charge of taking us to the warehouse for our G.I. (government issue) clothes and then to the dispensary for immunization shots.

We had just returned to the barracks with two

duffle bags of Army gear when Moore blew his whistle for us to fall in formation in front of the buildings for retreat, a ceremony signaling the lowering of the flag at sundown. At the end of the 10-minute ritual, we were told to fall out for chow (withdraw from formation to eat). The "veteran" recruits ran to be the first in line at the mess hall. By the time I figured out what was happening, I was about 200th in a line of 350 hungry men.

A young soldier standing in front of me fell to the ground. Luckily, someone standing nearby recognized that he was having an epileptic seizure and placed a stick in his mouth to prevent him from biting his tongue.

The first meal and the first night in the Army were uneventful, although I almost fell off the top of a double-deck bunk as I turned in my sleep. The next morning, we were awakened by a thundering voice on the loud speaker: "Ha, ha, ha, ha. I am The Shadow. Since The Shadow sees all and knows all, The Shadow can see you laying there on your big, Black ass. Ha, ha, ha, ha. Get up! Get up! Every swinging dick let your feet hit the floor and your ass hit the door for reveille."

That afternoon, as we stood at attention for retreat, 1st Sgt. Hammond and Major Peterson, inspected the troops. When they reached me, the major stopped and asked, "What's your name, soldier?"

"Pvt. Dempsey J. Travis," I replied.

Hammond reprimanded me: "Goddamit soldier, you always say 'sir' when you are speaking to an officer."

I replied, "Yes sir!"

Peterson then asked, "What did you do for a living as a civilian?"

"I was a musician, sir!"

A picture of Private Travis on his first Army furlough, in the fall of 1942. His mother is flanked by he and his father standing by their 1941 Buick in Washington Park.

"Did you get this soldier's name, sergeant?" the major inquired.

Hammond replied, "I did, sir." And they both

stepped briskly down to the center of the parade ground to take their position in front of the troops.

The next day, I was called to the orderly (office) room. "Soldier, you have been selected to be a member of the permanent personnel of the 1609 Service Unit," Hammond said.

That was my first break. I was thankful that I would be stationed at Fort Custer and that I could go home every weekend after I finished the 12-week basic training.

My second break came when I was asked to organize an orchestra to play for Friday and Saturday night U.S.O. dances in Battle Creek. The gig paid $3 a night per man.

Everything went smoothly until one Sunday Hammond asked me, "What did you bring me from your last trip to town?"

"What?"

Hammond responded harshly, "You heard me."

I asked, "What was I supposed to have brought you?"

"A pint of Old Grand Dad 90-proof whiskey every time you play a dance," he growled.

That meant that I would be giving Hammond one-third of my salary for the privilege of playing music. That was, as my father used to say, "too much sugar for a dime."

My pride and conscience would not permit me

to swallow those strong-arm tactics, and I immediately made the top of Hammond's "people-to-make-miserable" list. If the last train to Chicago left at 9:45 p.m., the sergeant would issue my pass to commence at midnight. On Thanksgiving, when a girlfriend came to visit me from Chicago, Hammond refused to let me leave the camp until midnight, when everything in town was closed, and restricted the pass to a 5 a.m. return for reveille.

Hammond was such a son of a bitch that on several occasions I took refuge in the non-commissioned officers' room and wept. The other option was to physically destroy Hammond. Giving in to that temptation would have meant I had not learned to refuse to fail.

The destruction of the spirit of Pfc. Dempsey J. Travis was on the top of Hammond's May agenda. When I returned to camp from a weekend pass to Chicago on May 10, 1943, the sergeant executed his most fiendish scheme—I was put under house arrest the moment I entered the barracks.

"Guards, you have made a mistake," I pleaded. "I am not late. I wasn't due back in camp until 0700." The two guards simply shook their heads and kept their hands on their guns.

After about an hour, Hammond walked in with a sardonic grin on his face and said, "I have orders in my hand to ship you directly to a port of embarkation." I felt that I'd just been ordered to take a shortcut to hell.

I knew Hammond finally had a noose around my neck and was about to pull the trap door. He instructed the guards: "Keep this soldier under close surveillance and don't consider this assignment complete until Travis is placed on the troop train, and the train is out of your sight."

"Attention!" a guard shouted. "Right face, forward march." The three of us stepped off to the train in cadence. Enroute, soldiers on the street stopped and stared at me as if I were a criminal. Hammond had won the first round but I refused to let him teach me to learn to fail by breaking my spirit and winning the fight.

The train was loaded with Black men who had just been released from the stockade (Army prison). Most of them had been convicted for being AWOL (absent without leave), desertion, or other military offenses. Sending soldiers overseas prematurely was one method of controlling and punishing the incorrigibles.

I had never been late from a weekend pass or missed bed check, but I had no chance to plead my case. Heading Sgt. Hammond's hate list was almost enough to make a Black man turn white.

DIARY OF A BLACK ALIEN

"THOSE GERMAN PRISONERS WOULDN'T EAT IF I ALLOWED YOU TO SIT NEAR THEM!"

7

CHAPTER

Camp Shenango

The sealed special orders under which I was shipped out of Fort Custer, Michigan must have read, "Designation hell," because that is what I found at Camp Shenango, Pa.

I did not realize the extent of discrimination in the Army until I arrived at Shenango. The naked viciousness of Jim Crow had not unclothed itself at Fort Custer.

From the moment we arrived at Camp Shenango, I was riveted with the notion that Blacks had no status, no rights, no dignity, and no claim to human treatment. The hellishness of Shenango was symbolized by the slimy black mud I stepped in up to my ankles when I got off the train. It was a smelly mud, it was a mud that consumed me emotionally without physically enveloping me. It was a mud that caused me to think of being buried alive in quicksand. A thought that, if prolonged, could drive a man mad.

Blacks comprised 10 percent of the soldiers at the huge military installation where thousands of soldiers were being processed to be shipped overseas. They kept us out of sight of the white soldiers as much as possible. Our barracks were about a mile and a half from the main gate, near the edge of the woods. The Negro living quarters were located in a Jim Crow Army ghetto, a perfect replica of racially segregated cities like Chicago, New York, Atlanta, and Pittsburgh.

Conditions for African Americans on the military base were deplorable. We could not use the PX (post exchange) or any of the recreational facilities which were reserved for "whites only." For Blacks there were no paved roads, just mud, and no movie theaters - just huts. I felt like I had suddenly been thrust back in time into one of my grandmother's horror stories about slavery times. Blacks at this Army camp were supposed to efface themselves, stay out of the way of white folks and literally ride in back of the bus. I often referred to Pennsylvania as "the Mississippi of the North."

The German prisoners of war at Camp Shenango enjoyed better treatment than Black American soldiers received. The POWs were allowed to

America had two Armies in World War II; A white one and a colored one. A white jail and a colored jail. A white military police force and a colored military police force - with a white commissioned officer.

use all of the white recreation facilities and ride in the front of the bus while Blacks were being treated worse than enemy aliens.

Army food at its best was bad. The chow served in the Black mess halls was worse. Some parts of the meal were not edible. Bad meat and under-cooked watery "shit on a shingle" (powdered eggs) were staples at breakfast. At every meal there was a new outrage.

On my third night at Shenango I went to the

mess hall for dinner and found soldiers jumping up and down on the tables, stomping on the food in their trays. Sgt. Hammond had sentenced me to a living hell, and I knew that I must give serious thought about ways and means to retain my sanity.

I couldn't escape through attending a movie or drinking a 3.2 (alcohol content) beer, because there were no such things in the "colored" section of the camp, and Blacks were not permitted in the white area except on official daytime business.

Black soldiers who needed medical attention were suspect if we showed our faces on the "white" side of the camp. Once I was sent to the hospital because I had hurt my foot on an obstacle course. A white, middle-aged doctor with the rank of a full colonel, asked me, without a smile or an examination, "Boy, what's your problem?"

"My right leg and foot are in pain, sir."

"Your what?"

"My leg and foot have been hurt, sir."

"Where is the blood, nigger?" the doctor asked.

"The injury is internal and didn't break the skin, sir."

"Boy!," he snarled, glaring at me, "a nigger's feet are supposed to hurt. Don't you show your Black face in this hospital again trying to goldbrick (avoid work) unless you're bleeding."

By my seventh week at Camp Shenango, the post authorities had begun to worry about racial conflicts that might result from the presence of the large number of Black soldiers being shipped into the replacement depot daily.

The immediate cause of their concern was that Blacks were trying to gain entrance to the white post exchanges and the white movie theaters and the realization that these young men needed something to do besides playing poker or blackjack, or shooting craps night and day.

The 332nd, an all Negro Fighter Group of pilots being briefed before a combat mission in Italy.

Some Black soldiers shot craps on doubled blankets spread out over the latrine floor where the lights were on 24 hours a day and within an arm's reach of men using the toilet. Sometimes the gamblers would shout in chorus, "Roll those dice, baby needs a new pair of shoes," or "Daddy needs some money to make honey with Bonnie." Occasionally a kneeling crap shooter would look up at a soldier sitting on the toilet and growl, "Cut it short and mix some water with that shit."

The morning of July 11, 1943, was hot and dusty. I said to Norman "Kansas" Taylor, my bunkmate who hailed from the Sunflower state. "Let's stay in the barracks and play cards until it's time to go to the movies and see Wuthering Heights, featuring Laurence Olivier and Merle Oberon."

"Okay," he said, "if the game is draw poker with a 5-cent limit."

Kansas was in good spirits and talked nonstop about his ambitions as we played cards. He had an undergraduate degree from an Eastern college and planned to go to medical school when he got out of the Army. My friend maintained his cheerful composure in spite of all the miseries of life at Camp Shenango. The only thing I ever heard him complain about was the commanding officer—white, of course—who refused to select him for A.S.T.P., an Army special training program that would have allowed him to enter medical school while still in the Army.

The hours passed quickly that Sunday. We didn't go to lunch because we heard that they were serving a dish we jokingly called "dear old billy goat" because it was always as tough as shoe leather. To this day, I believe we were being fed horse meat. At 5:30 we hit the chow line and then went to the make shift theater that had just been built almost overnight for Blacks. The line was already too long for us to catch the first show, so we discussed going into Sharon, a small town about 20 miles away.

Kansas was against it. "Let's wait until next Saturday and go into Youngstown (Ohio) where we can ball," he said. We played blackjack while waiting for the second show to start.

When we came out of the movie, a large group of Blacks was milling around in front of the theater. We went over to see what was going on.

"A Negro soldier had just got both eyes kicked out because he tried to buy a beer in the post exchange," we were told.

Another Black soldier screamed, "Let's go down there and get those cracker bastards!"

Kansas and I stared at each other, wondering what we should do. Before we could make a decision, six Army trucks pulled up, filled with white military police carrying M-1 rifles and double-barreled shotguns at the ready. On signal, the lights in the ghetto section of the post were turned out and the MPs opened fire on unarmed Black soldiers standing in the middle of the street. Kansas and I tried to break for cover, but it was too late. The screams and cries of soldiers who had been shot pierced the hot July night air.

I was knocked to the ground by a blunt force. I saw Kansas lying near me. I didn't realize I had been shot until I felt a warm, sticky substance soaking my pants leg and my shoulder. There was gunfire and confusion all around and over me, and then silence.

Several Army ambulances pulled up within minutes after the shooting stopped. Medics with flashlights stepped over the dead and wounded bodies lying as thick as flies on the dirt road. The medics were trying to determine who was dead, who was alive, who warranted a trip to the hospital or to the morgue. When they reached Kansas and me, they used their flashlights to motion for the stretcher-bearers.

"Can you walk?" a medic asked me.

I tried, but I was too numb to move. He turned me over and told another medic, "This nigger has been shot three times." Then, they turned their flashlights on Kansas. "They got this one in the stomach, but he'll be all right."

What did they mean? Did they mean he would be alright and I wouldn't? As I lay there preparing to die, my thoughts were not of heaven or hell. I was cursing the darkness. The blood oozing from my body was polluted with hate.

On the way to the hospital, I heard the ambulance driver say to the medic, "Why the hell do we shoot our own men?"

"Who said they were men?" the medic replied. "We shoot niggers like rabbits where I come from."

At the hospital, Kansas was rolled into a small room and I was left on a cart in the corridor. After a few minutes, a doctor rushed into the little room. I could see him lift my friend's eyelids. He put a stethoscope to his chest, then tried without success to straighten Kansas' bent legs. The doctor turned out the lights and closed the door.

Kansas was dead.

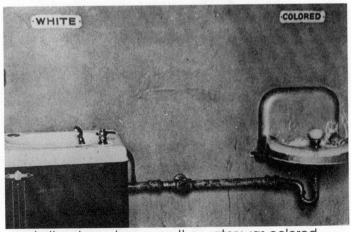

In the days when even the water was colored.

8

The Aftermath of a Sunday Night Bloodbath

I came out from under the comfort of some potent sedatives at daybreak Monday, only to be revisited by excruciating pains radiating from my gun shot wounds. I was momentarily distracted from my own misery by the groaning and cries of a ward full of young soldiers who had been wounded the night before in the Camp Shenango bloodbath. I learned later that the violence was still raging. As a matter of fact, it lasted three days after the Black soldiers broke into the supply depot and got guns and ammunition to protect themselves.

In the bed to my left was an eighteen-year-old kid screaming for his mother, his doctor, anybody. He thought he was dying. I tried to get out of my bed to console him, but discovered that the lower part of my body was paralyzed. I instantly joined the chorus of cries, screaming: "Help me! Help me! I can't move!"

Two orderlies rushed over to the bed and assured me that my paralysis was temporary.

"Don't worry," one said. "You will be all right."

The orderlies were brushed aside by an important-looking white man in a dark blue serge civilian suit, who said:

"Excuse yourself for a few minutes, I want to talk with this soldier."

He leaned over my bed and asked, in a soft voice, "How are you feeling this morning, young man?"

"Awful."

"Who shot you?" he said as he pulled a small black book from his inside jacket pocket and made several notations in it.

"What?" I asked.

"Did you have a gun?"

I didn't answer. I turned my head away from him in disgust. The man leaned closer. "Soldier, I'm here from the Intelligence Division in Baltimore, Maryland to help you," he whispered. "You must cooperate."

I turned my head back to look him straight in his saucer-shaped hazel eyes and said, "How?"

"I thought you might help me catch the radical

Communist trouble makers," he retorted.

"Mister, they were all white fascists dressed in the United States Army's green fatigues," I whispered. "Both the racist fascists and their smoking guns spoke with a Southern accent."

The man gave me a puzzled glance and made a few more notes and walked away.

Later on I was awakened from a drug induced nap by the voices of a team of doctors discussing my condition at the foot of my bed. Without saying anything to me, the physician in charge pulled the sheet off my body and gingerly turned me on my stomach and began jabbing his fingers in the center of my back just above the buttocks.

"Do you feel anything?"

"Yes, Sir!"

That response must have coincided with his prognosis, because he turned and said to the others, "He'll walk again."

The Camp Shenango riot didn't make any of the white daily newspapers in Chicago. The only way my parents found out what had happened to me was through the Red Cross. Mid-morning on Wednesday July 14, I spied my parents walking down the hospital corridor toward me. Dad was wearing his "I am the Boss" facial expression, the one that complemented his million-dollar stride. When Mother spotted me her face beamed like a well-lit Christmas tree.

I was literally choking in an effort to hold back the tears. Tears of joy at seeing my parents again mingled with tears of grief for my friend, Kansas, whose body was lying on a cold white slab in the hospital morgue waiting to be shipped in a flag-draped pine box to his family.

I was in worse shape than the doctors had led me to believe. My temperature was out of control, caused by an infection from the gunshot wounds. Therefore, they decided to ship me from the camp base hospital to DeShon Veterans General Hospital in Butler, Pa., which was a fifty-mile ride by ambulance from Shenango. I was told that I would be operated on there, however I was not told that I would be the only Black patient. I was given a private room on the top floor of the hospital. The first person to visit me was not a doctor, but the blue-suited man from the Intelligence Division I had met earlier at the base hospital in Shenango.

"I hope your trip was comfortable, and I'm sure you'll find this private room an improvement over the crowded ward back at the camp hospital," he said.

I nodded.

"Don't discuss the Shenango situation with anyone in the hospital. Do you understand?"

I nodded again. He raised his right hand, parted

his first and second fingers in a Winston Churchill "V for Victory" sign, said "good luck," and left the room.

My surgeon, Lt. Col. Richard Babcock, was a ruddy-faced, partially bald man with a very infectious and charming personality. Within a few days after I entered the hospital, he had me feeling as if he and I were in an undeclared war against the world. Col. Babcock knew my private room was not a privilege, but a prison in which to keep me quarantined to prevent the spread of a contagious virus called "niggeritis." He also knew that my operation could not be performed until the Red Cross was able to locate enough Negro Type "A" blood plasma in their segregated blood banks.

Moreover, the colonel was wise enough to know if I were ever able to escape from my hospital room, I would be treated as an untouchable by the white patients.

"Don't take any books or papers in that room, Mary. They put a "coon" in there last night who can't read or write," Those were the words that passed through the lips of a white woman hospital employee who was standing outside my partially closed room door. Several days later I caught a little white lady, less than five feet tall, in a Red Cross cap peeking into my room.

"Hello, there!" I said. "Won't you come in?"

She blushed, smiled sheepishly and stepped into the room, extending her hand.

"I'm Mary. I came up to see if we could do anything for you."

I don't know, but I would certainly like to get out of this bed."

After lunch the next day, Mary came up with a wheelchair that had been ordered by Dr. Babcock and offered to take me for a ride. In the corridor we got such stares of hatred and gasps of disapproval that I said, "Mary, let's go back to the room."

Mary was short in stature and weighed less than 100 pounds, but she had a lot of guts, she would not turn around. She returned daily to give me a ride after that first chilling experience. The stares and glares continued until one day she rolled my wheelchair down to the hospital auditorium, and I played a couple of jazz numbers on the piano during the recreation hour. After that I started to have some friends, and some of the white soldiers even began offering to replace Mary as my wheelchair pilot.

One day we were within 200 feet of my room when a tall, grim-faced soldier in a purple robe and white pajamas jumped into the path of the wheelchair with both arms stretched out like a traffic cop. The man grabbed the arms of the wheelchair, and both Mary and I almost panicked. He burst into a loud laugh. "My buddies and I have decided to take turns chauffeuring the piano player around," he said. The big soldier introduced himself as Pfc. James Messina from Newark, New Jersey. Mary thanked him for his offer, but added, "Soldier, you could have offered your services in a fashion that would have been less threatening."

Jim, who was one of eight children in a first generation Italian family, had completed his junior year at Rutgers University a month before he was drafted into the Army. Sometimes he would try to equate the prejudice against Italians with that against Blacks, but I kept telling him, "Jim, you can get that monkey off your back if you remove the vowel 'a' from the end of your name and change your church. Man, that would make you an instant WASP."

"Travis, you got the right name and the right church. The only thing wrong with you is your color," he said.

"Some of you Italians are dark enough to pass for colored," I would say when Jim tried to get too hip and I teased him that that might be because Hannibal and his Carthaginian troops from North Africa had occupied Italy for fifteen years from 218 B.C. to 203 B.C.

I had two successful operations, but the third was postponed several times. Lt. Col. Babcock and the other surgeon, Col. Cohen, disagreed over the risk involved in removing the bullet fragments from the lower part of my back. Babcock thought such an operation would cripple me permanently. Cohen disagreed. Babcock resigned from the case, and Col. Cohen went ahead and performed the operation—successfully.

After the last operation, I got a thirty-day leave to go to Chicago. My mother and I spent almost the entire period writing letters to President Franklin Delano Roosevelt, US Rep. William L. Dawson, US Senators Scott W. Lucas (Dem.) and C. Wayland Brooks (Rep.) in an effort to get an honorable discharge.

When I returned to the hospital in Butler, I was told I had been reassigned to Camp Shenango. I protested to Col. Cohen that I was still having trouble walking. He looked at me through his piercing eyes and said, "Soldier, that limp you have attempted to perfect in your right leg is a fake."

"Sir!" I protested. "It's excrutiating for me to have to walk on this leg."

"Don't worry, soldier," he said. "With your I.Q., you aren't going to have to walk. We're going to arrange for you to sit in a chair in this man's army for the duration."

It didn't work out quite like that, but it was close. When I got back to Shenango, I found that some changes had been made. The official name of the post had been changed to Camp Reynolds, and a large service club had been built in the black area of the camp. The color bars had been lowered, and Blacks were allowed to attend the main movie theater in the white area. All this was done to cleanse the air of the racist stench that had hovered over Shenango after the riot.

In June, 1944, after I had given up all attempts to get discharged from the Army, I was shipped to Camp Lee, Virginia.

The train that carried our troops had a three-hour layover in Washington, D.C., and I had a real opportunity to witness Jim Crow with no clothes on. Everything was racially separated, from water fountains to soda fountains. Even the taxicabs were segregated. Blacks could only ride in cabs owned or driven by other Blacks, and black cabs weren't permitted to enter the horseshoe curve in front of Union Station. Women, men and children had to carry their luggage a block from the station to reach any form of transportation that would accomodate colored people.

Racism and classism was so contagious in the District of Columbia that black people were practicing it on each other. On the Capital Transit, a circular advertising rooms for "light-colored folks only" was being distributed by a young man.

Roy Eldridge, the Black trumpet star with the Gene Krupa Orchestra, received double pay for not appearing with the band at the "For whites only" Lowe's Theater in Washington. The Howard Theater in the heart of the Black community on Florida Avenue was the only movie house with live, top-flight black stage shows. They featured such bands as Jimmy Lunceford, Claude Hopkins, Baron Lee, Lucky Millinder, Duke Ellington, Andy Kirk, Erskine Hawkin and Count Basie. I had seen all of those bands in Chicago and also with the U.S.O. shows during my tour at Camp Lee.

Duke Ellington played at Camp Lee when I was there. Left to right: Wellman Broad (bass), Toby Hardwick (saxophone), Duke Ellington, Lawrence Brown (trombone), Joe Nanton (trombone), Rex Stewart (trumpet), Arnie Whetsol (trumpet), Harry Carney (baritone sax), and directly behind Carney is Johnny Hodges, Juan Tizol (trombone), Fred Guy (guitar), Barney Bigard (sax and clarinet), Sonny Greer (drums). Cootie Williams (trumpet is on stage but is not shown. Rex Stewart (trumpet) is shown to the right of Sonny Greer at the top of the picture.

After the Washington exposure I didn't find Confederate Virginia as bad as I had expected. My survival mechanism made quick adjustments to a less than subtle form of American apartheid. I found the seats at the back of the bus and the "for colored only" waiting rooms in the train stations offensive, but not unbearable.

Back at the post, the black Army's heavily-shoed feet marched left-right, left-right, in the hot Virginia sun. The drill sergeant would lead the platoon in an ad-lib lyric to a World War I pop song:

"Virginia is a helluva state,
Parlez-vous;
"Virginia is a helluva state,
Parlez-vous;
"Virginia is a helluva state,
The asshole of the forty-eight,
Hinky, dinky parlez-vous."

As we continued our march, we would sing:

"They say this is a white man's war,
Parlez-vous;
"They say this is a white man's war,
Parlez-vous;
"They say this is a white man's war,
Well, what the hell are we fighting for?
Hinky, dinky parlez-vous."

The exhilaration of marching was instilling in me a positive attitude about going over to fight for a democracy that I or my people have never known. But I wasn't going. My high I.Q. score caused me to be selected to attend the Quartermaster School for Administrators at Camp Lee and then I was subsequently transferred to Aberdeen Proving Ground in Maryland, over my protests. The company commander told me he received a special order from Washington stating that I was to be sent to Maryland for the duration of the war, and not overseas.

Upon my arrival at Aberdeen, Major Sloan, the company commander asked me to organize a band for the company. I accepted the assignment with genuine joy.

"Good," he said, in his booming Texas accent. "You can do that in your spare time. Right now, I want you to type."

"Sorry, sir, I don't know how to type."

"Private Travis, you can learn." Major Sloan reached into his bottom desk drawer, pulled out a typing book, and handed it to me. Then he told the company clerk to give me a desk and a typewriter. Within thirty days I had become a self-taught fifty-words-a-minute typist. I credit my rapid progress to finger dexterity which I developed as a piano player.

Major Sloan did not feel the typing job was challenging enough for me, hence he promoted me to assistant manager of the Colored Post Exchange within ninety days of my arrival at Aberdeen, then manager, and finally I became area manager over three post exchanges, including the first large integrated post exchange in the state of Maryland. In that position, I won the first prize weekly award for the best-operated Post Exchange. I continued to win the weekly contest for two straight years. The Army took my picture, but did not run it in the post newspaper as was customary. The executive officer in charge of post exchanges told me, "Travis, we just can't afford to print this. It would offend too many people. I hope you understand."

So my Army career ended in relative prosperity: I got a promotion to Technical Sgt. Fourth Grade,

Aberdeen Proving Grounds, 1944: Dempsey J. Travis pictured in the A.P.G. Exchange with award he retained for 2 years for operating the best Post Exchange. This picture was never published in the Post newspaper because the company commander said it would cause racial tension.

and, along with the bi-weekly salary I received as exchange manager, I was making double my sergeant's pay. My father was a great lover of cigars, and I used to send him at least two boxes of the best smokes each month.

I frequently thought about him back in Chicago, smoking my cigars and bragging to the neighbors about his son. I was looking forward to the day when I could return home and enjoy the company of my mother and father.

In the meantime I had adopted New York's Harlem as my new home for most of my weekend passes.

I recall one night at Smalls Paradise on 135th and 7th Avenue in Harlem. I must have put over forty nickels in the jukebox to hear the Mills Brothers and Ella Fitzgerald's rendition of "Into Each Life Some Rain Must Fall." I played that song over and over again and my friend Phil Pruitt said, "Man, aren't you tired of hearing that song?"

I replied, "For some unknown reason I can't stop playing it."

Phil said, "Are you having trouble with your old lady?"

"Nope!" I replied, "but I think I will call my mother. I haven't talked to her for two months."

I placed a collect call to Chicago and the first thing my mother said was, "Where are you? I have been calling Aberdeen trying to reach you for two days to tell you we had to rush your father to the County Hospital."

I hung up the phone abruptly and called Master Sgt. Morris Brown for a special pass to go to Chicago. He told me I could go directly from New York and that he would mail my furlough papers to my home. I caught the New York Central's "Pacemaker" that afternoon and arrived in Chicago on Saturday morning, December 16, 1944.

I went directly from the train station to Cook County Hospital. Dad's fear of the County Hospital and its alleged "black bottle" for colored folks meant he had to have been critically ill to consent to going there. My arrival at Dad's bedside confirmed my suspicions. They had needles and tubes hooked into his arms and his nose. I had been in the ward for more than an hour when Dad opened his eyes, beckoned for me to come closer, then touched the sergeant's stripes on my Army uniform, smiled without saying a word and closed his eyes again.

Since Dad was on the critical list the intern permitted me to sit by his bed throughout the night. The only sound Dad made all night came from a heavy roaring in his chest. At 5:48 a.m. Sunday morning he opened his eyes and said, "I didn't think you would get here in time." I didn't respond. I simply touched his hand and smiled. Dad looked at me through his weak, watery eyes and said in a soft but audible voice, "Boy! Take care of your mother." Seconds after he spoke those words his eyes seemed to roll back into his head, and his mouth snapped open as if his jawbone had become unhinged. My father was pronounced dead at 6:03 a.m. Sunday, December 17, 1944.

Our Allied Armies had pulled up along the German Siegfried line in December, 1944, when Hitler launched his fanatical counter-offensive of the war. So effective was the Germans' offensive that the Allied troops were forced back some fifty miles, almost to the sea.

The tides turned in January, 1945, when the Allies retaliated with a renewed offensive. The Soviets had also begun a winter offensive. By the end of February, the Soviet allied troops had moved westward within thirty miles of Berlin. The American and British troops were advancing eastward. Victory for the Allied troops was in the air when President Franklin D. Roosevelt died suddenly on April 12th, 1945, in Warm Springs, Georgia. Although most Blacks had been denied the right to cast a vote for Roosevelt in the four times he was elected President, they reacted to his death as one would react to the loss of a close friend or relative. (Roosevelt served less than three months in his fourth term.)

I arrived in Washington, D.C. from Aberdeen,

Maryland, on Saturday, April 14th, to visit with relatives over the weekend. The train station was jammed with dignitaries of all types awaiting the 10:30 a.m. arrival of the Roosevelt Funeral Train. Black and white folks stood integrated on both sides of the streets, sidewalk deep, from the train station to the Capitol. Many of them were openly weeping. It was heartbreaking to stand there among a throng of Blacks and Whites who had become unified in tears over a fallen leader. The vibrations of my heartbeat seemed louder than the clop, clop from the hoofs of the six white horses that pulled the caisson carrying President Roosevelt's flag-covered coffin. The moans from the crowd as the coffin passed were subdued by the drone of planes overhead, and the humming from the motors of the slow moving black limousines.

The War moved swiftly over the next twenty-five days. The German government surrendered unconditionally at General Eisenhower's headquarters on May 7, and May 8, 1945, was declared as V-E (Victory in Europe) Day. Less than 120 days after Roosevelt's death, President Harry S. Truman issued an ultimatum to the Japanese to surrender or face "prompt and utter destruction." Truman waited a week and on August 6th, 1945, his promise of destruction fell out of the sky in the epoch-making event of an atomic bomb being dropped on the city of Hiroshima in Japan. The city was obliterated: 75,000 to 80,000 people were killed, and thousands more permanently injured. On August 14, Japan agreed to surrender. One hundred and fifty days later, on February 2, 1946, I surrendered my uniform at Indiantown Gap, Pa. The captain at the "Gap" separation center told us that we had thirty days to get out of uniform and into civilian clothes. Within thirty hours after I left the "Gap" I was back in Chicago standing on the corner of 47th and South Parkway in a ready-made double-breasted cocoa brown suit. The real world that I was about to grapple with was unlike the civilian utopia I dreamed about during my forty months and twenty-three days stay in the Army.

47th and South Parkway (King Drive) on a typical Sunday afternoon during the 1930s and 40s. Note the long line of patrons waiting to get into the Regal Theatre.

The Regal Theater had a Louis XIV castle appearance and was the center along with the Savoy Ballroom for Black entertainment in Chicago from 1927 through the early 1950s (the theatre was shamefully demolished in the late 1970s). Black entertainemnt attractions such as Duke Ellington, The Mills Brothers, Cab Calloway, The Ink Spots, and Jimmie Lunceford appeared regularly at the Regal. The author personally witnessed lines of people waiting to see these and other artists that sometimes stretched four abreast, from the box office at the middle of 47th Street and South Parkway (King Drive) for a block and a half to 47th Street and Vincennes. The Regal Theater was an entertainment institution in the Black community. The destruction of the Regal caused a cultural void in the Black community until a New Regal Theater was opened by Edward and Bettiann Gardner at 79th and Stony Island - a decade and a half later.

9

CHAPTER

Education: A Ladder From the Bottom to the Top

"Black boy! You can't read, you can't write, and you can't calculate. Your future lies in the class of the hard laborer, performing tasks that require a strong back and an unlettered mind."

Those were not the exact words in the rejection letters I had received from Roosevelt, DePaul and Northwestern universities after I returned home from the Army, but they might as well have been. In essence, their messages were the same: I had failed the entrance examinations at each of those institutions. My disappointments were deep because I knew I had the intellectual equipment in that I had achieved more than a modicum of success in the music business in Chicago prior to World War II, as well as in the Jim Crow United States Army, where I was programmed to be physically and mentally destroyed.

The suspicion that the rejections might have had more to do with racism than with my academic potential was of no comfort. I knew that DePaul and Northwestern had strict quotas for both Blacks and Jews.

I could not blame quotas for being turned down by Roosevelt because the college was quota-free. The college emerged on April 17, 1945, in protest to the bigotry at the Central YMCA College. The initial protest took place when Dr. Edward J. Sparling, president of the college, refused to give the board of trustees of the college a Black head count that would enable them to establish quotas for the educationally starved Black veterans returning from World War II. The racial climate at Central YMCA College was such that they also charged Blacks recreational fees for facilities they were not permitted to use, such as the swimming pool and other physical education equipment.

In 1946, Roosevelt College was a beacon of hope for Black war veterans, and many of my buddies rushed downtown to 231 South Wells to enroll.

I was left out. My ambitions and the new sense of adulthood that I had brought back from four years in the Army could not compensate for the fact that I

Above left: Roosevelt College was located at 231 S. Wells St. in 1945. Upper right: President Franklin Delano Roosevelt, who died April 12, 1945. Lower right: College President Dr. Edward J. Sparling and Eleanor Roosevelt, President Roosevelt's widow, at the college dedication ceremony in November 1945.

failed to prepare for college while sailing through high school with my mind on music instead of general academic studies.

Those notices from the universities convinced me that my refusal to take my elementary and high school lessons seriously had extracted a toll on my future, therefore I had no option other than accepting a laborer's job in the Union stockyard at Armour and Company.

The entrance to the Union Stockyards, the headquarters for the hog butchers of the world.

In March 1946, I decided to take a chance on self-employment. I had taken a correspondence course in accounting during my Army years, and decided that an alternative to backbreaking labor would be to set myself up as a tax consultant. I quit the stockyards and my first clients were members of a storefront church at 2216 South State Street where my cousin, Rev. Victoria Pitts, was the pastor.

Working with tax returns gave me so much confidence that I decided to take two courses at Englewood Evening Junior College where there were no entrance requirements and the registration fee was only $5. With the encouragement of a high school friend, Dustalear Cook, who had become a public schoolteacher while I was away at war, I passed both courses with better than a "B" average.

The summer of 1946 led me into a more ambitious venture. I leased the ballroom in the Pershing Hotel at 64th and Cottage Grove for four dance dates. I booked a famous recording act, the "Cats and the Fiddle," headed by the very popular Austin Powell, a DuSable High School alumnus, for the first date.

It was a flop. My partner, a man I admired because he had a college degree from a university, sold only 30 tickets to the dance. I sold 390 tickets. I quickly decided that I did not need a colleague who could not sell hot dogs at a football game and we agreed to dissolve our association, and sell the three remaining dates to the Adams brothers, two successful local dance promoters.

I was more determined than ever after the dance promotion experience to get a college degree. I took the placement examination at Wilson Junior College (now Kennedy-King) and was informed I would have to take remedial reading and English. Not understanding just what I was letting myself in for, I registered for American Literature 117 as an elective.

On the very first day, Dr. Whitney E. Smith, the remedial reading class instructor, paced back and forth in the front of the lecture hall and delivered a little speech that has echoed in my ears ever since:

"Now, I think I should start this class by telling you that if you have gone this far in life and still have to be assigned to a remedial reading class, you'd just better face the fact that you're not going to make it in college. The cards of academic life have been stacked against you. My statistics show that only one out of every 200 students who have enrolled in this class within the past 10 years, graduate from this college with an Associates of Art Degree. Eighty-five percent of you present today will not survive the first college year here at Wilson."

Smith's statement set my brain whirling with the prospect that I would be that one out of 200 in our class who would graduate. But the grandiose promises that I had made to myself bumped sharply against the reality of my inability to read. Oh, sure,

I could muddle through job application forms, letters and daily newspapers. But when more sophisticated reading, like wading through thick textbooks, was required, I floundered.

I struggled painfully through high school-level texts, reading every page one word at a time. But in the "lit" class, we were required to write a comprehensive report on a different book each week. I quickly discovered that this was over my head. I spent 10 to 20 minutes on a single page, and I stayed up until 3 and 4 o'clock in the morning to complete my assignments.

"Why don't you go to bed, boy, and get some sleep?" my mother would plead.

"Mama, there is no time to sleep. I have got to learn to read."

"Boy, you're ruining your health," she admonished.

"Mama, how can I have a healthy body with a malnourished mind? A man is what he eats and a mind is what it reads."

"Suit yourself," she would answer as I returned to wrestling with the literary classics of Nathaniel Hawthorne, Henry Thoreau, and Sinclair Lewis.

When Dr. Ernest Ernst, the literature instructor, read my first book report, he threatened to throw me out of the class. He thought my paper was some kind of joke. I convinced him that it was not and told him

I was willing to redo the report as many times as necessary, until he found it acceptable. He agreed to let me stay in the class provided I came to his office three afternoons a week to review my progress.

"Dr. Ernst, what did I do wrong?" I asked on my first visit.

He shook his head. "Well, you just didn't understand what you read. Why don't you try again?"

I had no resentment. I just kept trying.

About the sixth week into the semester it paid off. I was inching through a book by Theodore Dreiser, one word and one phrase at a time, when suddenly it clicked! It became clear—it all fell into place. The words rolled together into sentences, and the sentences rolled into paragraphs and the paragraphs uncoiled into pages of thoughts and ideas.

My elated yell from discovering early one morning just before dawn that I had learned to read caused my mother to tumble out of her bed and come running down the hall. She thought I had had a stroke.

"Great God a'mighty, Mama, I can read!" I shouted.

But there was another handicap to overcome. It was almost impossible for me to express myself logically on paper. If Dempsey couldn't read, you can be certain he was unable to write.

In December of 1947, I was trying to compose a

letter to the Veterans Administration to explain that I had never received a disability check for the suffering caused by the gunshot wounds I received during the race riot at Camp Shenango.

Suddenly another miracle occurred. Like magic, I discovered I had written eight pages in less than an hour, describing, giving reasons, and drawing conclusions. Before this breakthrough, it would have taken me an hour to compose two poorly constructed paragraphs.

I had learned to read, and simultaneously I had learned to write! I was 27 years old, and at that age the discovery of the potency of the written page was euphoric. Unearthing the potential of a mature mind is a powerful force for change.

My studies suddenly became easier. In spite of the negative influences surrounding me, I retained my good spirits and fought past all the obstacles. Most of the students in the remedial reading class did not hurdle the barriers and learned to fail during that first academic year, as Dr. Smith had predicted. I succeeded because I had subconsciously adopted an "I refuse to learn to fail" philosophy.

It was the refuse to learn to fail spirit that propelled Jackie Robinson to run the bases of liberation for Black America when he was called to play in the major leagues April 9, 1947. And it was that same spirit that rocketed me through Wilson Junior College in 16 months instead of the usual 24. I received my diploma on January 30, 1948, along with my friend, Congressman Gus Savage.

My diploma was a quick passport to Roosevelt University, which Black students hailed as the fountainhead of democracy in higher education. Of course, Roosevelt had no competition in the democracy sweepstakes from other universities and colleges whose doors were closed, except on a token basis, to people of color.

In 1948, the spirit of brotherhood that permeated the university was unlike anything I had experienced. Every morning when I stepped inside the university I was enveloped with a feeling of hope for Black Americans. But, each afternoon when I stepped outside onto Michigan Avenue, I was jarred back to the realization that Roosevelt University did not mirror the real world.

Daily, as I walked north on Michigan to catch an almost-empty bus going south, I looked at the tall, white-owned office buildings and said, "Those buildings don't even have black smoke coming out of the chimney." I knew that Blacks did not have a "toenail hold" on the financial fortunes of America, and I dedicated myself to challenging the status quo, which was simply unacceptable to me. At the time I believed the vehicle for accomplishing my goal would be through classes in law and politics.

At Roosevelt I studied with some mighty bright young Blacks: Gus Savage; Harold Washington; Oscar Brown Jr., composer, actor, producer and singer; Robert L. Kimbrough and Clarence Towns, now dentists; Frank London Brown, author of a novel on Trumbull Park; and Mark Jones, Circuit Court Judge, Cook County, Illinois. One evening in May 1948, Savage, Washington, Oscar , Frank, Bennett Johnson and I argued as we sat on the floor in a temporary trailer housing park for veterans at 57th and Perry, the home of Gus and Eunice Savage. We finally agreed, after much debate, on a Black agenda. One of the planks in the agenda was that both Gus Savage and Harold Washington should run for Congress. Gus agreed to run from a West Side district and Harold agreed to run from the South Side.

It took 32 years to fulfill a commitment that sounded like a "pork dieter's" dream. The six men who sat on the floor that night were dreamers all right, dreamers who continued to support one another financially and spiritually after graduating from Roosevelt University in August 1949.

Our dedication and determination were rewarded with more famine than feast until January of 1981, when Gus Savage and Harold Washington were sworn into the U.S. Congress as representatives of the 1st and 3rd Illinois Districts, respectively.

The First District Congressman Charles A. Hayes was a director of District 1 for the United Packing House Workers of America, C.I.O. He is shown in 1955, delivering a pre-strike rally speech on the main street of the Union Stockyards.

10

CHAPTER

Black Pepper in Hard Times

In September 1949, I married Moselynne Hardwick, entered Chicago Kent Law School and began a career in real estate that has spanned more than four decades.

The autumn of 1949 was the worst of times to go into business. The economy was down and the unemployment lines were long. Although Moselynne had a job at Encyclopedia Britanica, conditions were so bad that for 13 weeks, I shared a one-room office rent-free with attorney William Hughes.

We used the closet-sized space on the second floor of the Old State Theater building at 3509 South State like a hot bed: Hughes held office hours from 9:00 a.m. until 2:00 p.m. Monday through Friday, when I attended law school. I occupied the facility in the afternoon when he went to work as a fulltime postal clerk. The attorney generously agreed that I wouldn't have to pay rent until I had earned my first real estate commission.

I did not earn a single dollar in commission during those three months, and there were no prospects fighting for my attention. In December, Hughes moved across the street into the Binga Arcade building to share offices with several other lawyers who also worked full-time at the post office. Hughes left without notifying me, taking his desk and chairs, the telephone and phone directory. He didn't even leave the calendar on the wall.

To avoid inhabiting a totally naked office I used an orange crate from the corner grocery store as a desk and a rusty tin scrub bucket donated by the building janitor for a chair. I began to understand what my parents meant when they said that hard times would make me eat black pepper.

On the rare occasions when I had an appointment with a client, attorney Horace Galloway, who had subleased the office to Hughes, permitted me to use his suite. One day Dr. Allen L. Wright, a physician who had been a 1939 DuSable High School classmate, paid me a surprise visit. He found real estate broker Dempsey J. Travis sitting on a water pail behind a orange crate, but Wright displayed no surprise at what must have been a comical sight.

"What do you have to sell in Douglas Park?" he asked.

"I have a deluxe yellow brick three flat, with

three six-room apartments with double plumbing in each unit, at 1641 South Drake Avenue."

"That sounds like something I might be interested in. When can I see it?"

"Any time you want. But we'll have to take the streetcar because I don't own a car," I confessed. Dr. Wright drove us to the building.

A few days later the doctor and his wife Alyce inspected the property. They bought it: my first sale! My commission of $1,240 was more money than I had ever possessed at any one time in my life.

When Moselynne came home from work that evening she spied the big check in the middle of the bed, where I had placed it so she couldn't miss it.

"Baby, you can quit your job now and come home and take care of our business," I crowed.

Moselynne's office skills proved a real asset to our enterprise. Each day, she typed 40 or more letters, 20 to residents in the Douglas Park area, soliciting property for sale, and an equal number to selected residents in the Lake Meadows area. Some 3,416 homeowners and tenants in the 100-acre site were being displaced by the urban renewal program implemented by the city of Chicago and the New York Life Insurance Company. The properties stretched north to south from 31st to 35th streets and from South Park on the west to the Illinois Central Railroad tracks on the east. Many of these families, who received between $3,000 to $5,000 for their equity from The Department of Urban Renewal, used the money for a down payment on West Side properties. My wife and I became very good at matching South Side people with Douglas Park housing.

Jewish residents in the Douglas Park neighborhood regarded the Black South Side immigrants with equanimity, unlike the Irish, Italian and Polish people in the East Woodlawn, Park Manor and Chatham communities who reacted violently to what they perceived as a "Black invasion" of Southeast Chicago. The Jewish homeowners in Douglas Park were so cordial that I sometimes mustered enough nerve to ask why they were moving.

Their answers were the same: "We're moving west to California."

I thought it was strange that so many people from the same area would be moving to the West Coast. Years later, a Jewish friend told me that "California" was their nickname for Skokie, Ill. Jewish sellers in Hyde Park who moved north to Rogers Park, Lake Shore Drive, Skokie and Highland Park were fond of telling me that they were moving to Florida.

Searching out mortgage financing for Blacks dispossessed by urban renewal in 1950 and 1951 was more exhausting than driving a mule train non-stop from Chicago to California. The mule train might ultimately reach its destination, but not every dis-

placed Black family could find a home for a mortgage loan.

The major white-owned banks and savings
and loan associations in the Loop were not interested
in making loans to African American borrowers.
Chicago's two small Black-owned savings and loan
associations didn't have enough money to meet the
demand. Angry whites publicly protested at City
Hall against proposed subsidized housing for low-
income Blacks uprooted by urban renewal.

White speculators had no trouble obtaining
mortgage money from Black life insurance companies and savings and loan associations to exploit the
Black home buyers via contract sales. It was common
for Blacks to buy homes on contract from speculators

*Members, family, and friends of the Contract Buyers League burn a facsimile
of a real estate contract belonging to Charles Davis, a contract buyer and Co-
Chairman of the Contract Buyers League. The ceremony was held to com-
memorate the first mortgage financed under the Contract Buyers' agreement
coordinated by Dempsey J. Travis.*

who had acquired them with a 100% mortgage and then marked up the price by 200- to 300 %.

Contract selling to Blacks was a common practice in Chicago into the early 1970s. A successful lawsuit filed by the Westside and the Southside Contract Buyers' leagues dampened the practice. The land contract is intrinsically a good document, but was so exploited by white and Black speculators that the instrument was tainted with a slaveship stench.

Exploitation in any form is vicious. Exploiting an economically and culturally disadvantaged people in their efforts to seek basic food and shelter is vile. I refused to become a "bird dog" for white speculators who plundered the Black housing market with Black and white loans.

I had been a licensed broker on a survival diet for almost a year before I met Henry Banach, a Polish gentleman, and August Saldukus, a Lithuanian. Through Banach, I procured loans for Blacks at the Polish-controlled Universal Savings and Loan Association on the city's Near Southwest Side. Saldukus was president of the Midland Savings and Loan Association, which was located in the heart of the Lithuanian Community. During my first years in the business, these two institutions made 99 percent of my loans. I was delighted with the arrangements, because they enabled my people to obtain deeds instead of contracts. Both institutions charged a 5 percent service fee plus 6 percent interest annually.

These service charges were bargains, since the bandit lenders demanded a 10 percent under-the-table cash service fee up front, plus 6 percent per annum.

The magnitude of the discrimination in the mortgage market was obvious. White buyers during that period paid an average service charge of 1 percent or less, with an interest rate that hovered slightly above 5 percent. Some major institutions paid white brokers a 1 percent finders' fee for every white borrower who qualified for a mortgage.

The oppressive effect of discrimination convinced me that the only way a Black man could survive in real estate and serve his people would be to funnel the dormant monies held by major white insurance companies and pension funds into the Black neighborhoods. The newly organized Sivart Mortgage Corporation would be the conduit to achieve that objective.

Sivart, as a mortgage banking institution with its roots, purposes and dreams in the African American community, could tap the billions being held by white institutions. Implementing the concept against many tough obstacles consumed almost a decade.

In 1951, Chicago was a city deeply divided by racist practices so severe that my friends shook their heads and said I was hopelessly out of step when I spoke of my mortgage banking dream. In those days, Black minds in America were wired to one report after another of racial violence in the North

The Clark family was never able to take possession of the apartment in Cicero. Shown making a presentation to the Clark family is Willard Townsend, national vice president of the NAACP, standing at the extreme right. Nelson M. Willis, left, and Attorney John W. Rogers, (currently a circuit court judge in the county of Cook) second from the right, look on. Little Michelle Clark, bottom left, later became the first black female national correspondent for CBS Television.

and in the South.

On June 8, 1951, Harvey Clark Jr., a Tuskegee Airman in World War II, ventured into the suburb of Cicero, the most vehemently defended bastion of white racism in the Chicago metropolitan area. Clark and Maurice Scott Sr., who owned the van that moved the Clark family's belongings, were greeted by several members of the Cicero Police Department when they arrived at 6139 19th Court, where Clark had rented a third-floor apartment.

"You niggers have no moving permit, and you can't move your nigger junk into this building," was their "Welcome Wagon" salute.

In the middle of the afternoon, George C. Adams, Clark's attorney, a Creole of black, French and Indian ancestry, received a telephone call from the janitor at the Cicero building. The janitor told him the police had halted Clark's move-in. Adams contacted Maurice Scott Jr. and the two lawyers sped away in Adams' car.

When the auto pulled up at the Cicero address, Scott saw a policeman holding a gun to the back of his father's head and kneeing him forward in the buttocks. Maurice ran over to them, and another Cicero cop put a gun to his head, while several middle-aged white women crowded around and spit in his face.

Clark and Adams, with the aid of two attorneys for the National Association for the Advancement of Colored People (NAACP), Ulysses S. Key and George M. Leighton, obtained an injunction against the Cicero police from U.S. federal Judge John P. Barnes. The injunction allowed Clark to move his furniture into the apartment but it did not abate the racist rage in the breast of the Cicero mob.

Only a small knot of whites watched as the Clarks moved in July 10, but by 9:30 the following night, the onlookers had grown to a growling mob of some 5,000 people, more than half of them women. During the night, teenage hoodlums broke into the building and threw the Clark's furniture, clothing, and other personal property out of the windows. Each time a window was broken or an object was hurled out, the mob would roar in delight. The roars amplified when the rioters symbolically lynched the Clarks by setting fire to the furniture and clothing that had been thrown to the ground. The Clarks were never allowed to occupy that apartment.

By the second night, the atmosphere in Cicero was one of a raw carnival without masks, a pack of wild white wolves in search of a collective organism that was stimulated by racial hatred. While the mob was there, howling and jeering on the third night, Police Chief Konovsy and his men left the scene, abandoning the Clark's possessions to the mercy of the good white citizens of Cicero.

Law and order for Black America had failed again.

Finally, at the urging of Alderman Archibald Carey and the Cook County Sheriff, Governor Adlai Stevenson sent in the National Guard to quell the disorder. It took 500 bayonet-wielding guardsmen to end the incident. This was the first time since the bloody Chicago riot of the summer of 1919 that a governor was forced to send troops into Cook County. A $200,000 lawsuit was filed in federal court against Cicero's town officials for violating the constitu-

National Guardsmen in fighting gear during Cicero Riot, 1951.

tional civil rights of the Scotts, the Clarks, and the Edwards.

The protective umbrella of the National Association for the Advancement of Colored People's bold civil rights efforts was one of the reasons I became a life member of that organization in the fall of 1952. Paying out a lump sum of $500 for membership in those dark economic days was not a small gesture for me—or for the NAACP. The organization had only 88 fully paid life members and 133 subscribing life members in 1953, compared with approximately 100,000 fully paid life members and 33,000 subscribing life members in 1991.

The occasion was the annual NAACP Freedom Fund Dinner held on June 17, 1960 at the Morrison Hotel in downtown Chicago. Left to right are Dempsey J. Travis, president of the NAACP; Cora Carroll, mayor of Bronzeville; and Thurgood Marshall, NAACP Chief Counsel and recently retired Associate Justice of the United States Supreme Court.

CHAPTER

Jim Crow Feels the Judicial Winds of Change

On May 17, 1954, the U.S. Supreme Court unanimously ruled in favor of public school desegregation in _Brown_ v. _Board of Education of Topeka, Kan._ The court finally dismantled the old "separate but equal" principle that was enshrined in the 1896 _Plessy_ v. _Ferguson_ decision.

Following that landmark ruling, I reasoned that the principle affecting education could also be applied to the intensively segregated housing market. In the 1950s, when many Blacks sought solutions to racism through integration, I believed a mobile housing market for minorities would pave the way for a color blind society. The four decades between 1951 and 1991 have proven that that notion was not valid, in that laws may integrate bodies but relatively few minds that have been nurtured in racism from birth by racist parents have been integrated.

The desire to bury our Black identity was very strong in the 1950s. The board of directors of the National Negro Business League at its 1954 convention held at the Parkway Ballroom in Chicago seriously considered deleting the word "Negro" from its title. The Chicago branch of the Negro Chamber of Commerce split into two bodies, the integrated Cosmopolitan Chamber of Commerce and the all-black Negro Chamber of Commerce.

Civil Rights and Business organizations searching for a new identity received positive signals from both the east coast and west coast establishments. In the east, it was from our seat of government in Washington, D.C., and in the west, it was our image makers in Hollywood, Calif.

From Washington, the winds of change for the nation were measured in three U.S. Supreme Court decisions: removal of the restrictive housing covenants in 1948, desegregation in railway dining cars in 1950 and desegregation of public schools in 1954. In 1949, President Harry S. Truman ordered the Army to integrate the races, a policy subsequently followed by both the Navy and the Air Force.

During the same period, "Black Sambo", "Farina" and "Amos & Andy" images were under attack in Hollywood by the NAACP. Clarence Brown's film adaptation of William Faulkner's "Intruder in the Dust," starring Juano Hernandez, shot on location in Oxford, Miss., presented the Black American in a positive image—one that had never been shown on an American screen. "Dust" was followed in 1956 by "Young Man with a Horn," which co-starred Hernandez and Kirk Douglas. A series of movies featuring Sidney Poitier appeared to indicate that America was finally ready to integrate, yet flare-ups of racial violence throughout the country dampened that optimistic outlook.

Sidney Poitier, the night he won the Academy Award's Oscar for his starring role in "Lillies of the Field". The 1964 event marked the first time a Black Actor had received the honor.

On August 28, 1955, Emmett Louis Till, a 14-year-old boy from Chicago, was taken at pistol point from his uncle's home in Money, Miss. The child was kidnapped by Roy Bryant and his half brother, J.W. Milam, for allegedly making a "wolf whistle" at Mrs. Bryant, an incident the two men alleged had occurred four days earlier. Till's water-swollen body, with one side of his face beaten to a pulp, a bullet hole in his head and a cotton gin fan lashed to his feet, was fished out of the Tallahatchie River near Green-wood, Miss., three days after he was kidnapped. Till was the 575th lynching victim recorded in Missis-sippi since 1882.

The all-white jury, manifesting no more thought for a Black boy's life than they might have given to a wild rabbit's, acquitted Bryant and Milam of the murder and kidnapping, even though the defendants admitted taking the boy from his uncle's home. Deputy U.S. Attorney William P. Rogers said in a television interview, "We just have no authority to step into a state even if we think there is a failure in the administration of justice."

This was a time when even the smallest acts of everyday living might call upon a Black person's deepest reserves of courage and heroism. Along with many other Americans, I drew strength from heroes such as Martin Luther King Jr. Dr. King's moving oratory generated the adrenaline that moved thousands to protest publicly but passively and work actively in the civil rights movement.

The social revolution that followed after Ms. Parks' arrest on December 1, 1955, in Birmingham, Ala., transformed America's virulent racism into a more subtle form of violence. Dr. King and many of his followers paid the full price for their commitment, they were killed. Black and white people gave their lives so that little Black girls and boys, in the North and the South, would never have to raise the question asked in the poem of my late friend, Langston Hughes:

"Where is the Jim Crow section
On this merry-go-round
Mister, cause I want to ride?
Down South where I come from
White and colored
Can't sit side by side.
Down South on the train,
There's a Jim Crow car.
On the bus we're put in the back.
But there ain't no back
To a merry-go-round!
Where's the horse
For a kid that's black?"

Fighting the Black housing problem in 1955 could best be described as riding on a merry-go-round at an accelerated speed. I scrambled around the clock seven days a week trying to remove the obstacles pushed onto the Black community by a mortgage market that was anchored in racism.

I felt very alone in my struggle until I met George S. Harris, president of the National Association of Real Estate Brokers, a Black real estate organization. Realtist was a counterpart to the National Association of Real Estate Boards, known as Realtors, a society which excluded Blacks from membership until 1963.

"Travis," Harris told me in the fall of 1955, "your efforts are like a minnow trying to change the tide of the ocean. I'll show you how we can lick this problem if you join the NAREB and become a part of an organized effort that's fighting for democracy in housing."

I accepted his challenge and went to New York that year to an NAREB convention. There I met many successful young Black realtists, among them was Q.V. Williamson of Atlanta, Ga., who became the first Black elected to the Atlanta Board of Aldermen since Reconstruction; William Harps of Washington, D.C., who in the 1980s became the first Black president of the American Institute of Real Estate Appraisers; and S.B. Odell of Oakland, Calif., a wealthy real estate developer and broker. We were all from different sections of the country but shared a common goal—democracy in housing.

I returned from the conference fired up by the idea of transforming the Dearborn Real Estate Board, the Chicago affiliate of the NAREB, into a powerful voice for Black housing in the Chicago metropolitan area. I was impatient. The slow parliamentary pace of the group irritated me. I couldn't help but think that the organization could become mummified while we were exercising ourselves over Robert's Rules of Order.

We needed new leadership and an active plan to deal with racism in housing, but the group was very much bound to tradition and their own way of doing things. For instance, it was the custom for the first vice president to succeed to the presidency of the board, even if that person displayed a total absence of leadership qualities.

The day before the annual election in the fall of 1957, I polled the "young Turks" in the group for support for my own candidacy for the presidency. The old guard was surprised and displeased when I won by two votes. They thought my intrusion into established procedures was rude and rash. I insisted that rudeness and rashness are sometimes necessary when confronting pervasive problems like racism in the housing market and inertia in a professional organization.

My first five months in office were hell. Some members threatened to resign from the board. There was no staff. I used my own staff and financial resources, not exactly those of a Rockefeller at the time. The tide turned in May 1958, when four Travis Realty sales associates and I packed the Parkway

Frank London Brown was the speaker at the first installation banquet of Dempsey J. Travis as President of the Dearborn Real Estate Board.

Photographed in 1957, are left to right: George S. Harris, President, National Association of Real Estate Brokers; Dempsey J. Travis, President, Dearborn Real Estate Board presenting award to the late Elmore Baker, Founder of the Dearborn Real Estate Board; following the the unidentified gentleman to the right of Baker is Attorney George Crank, the late J. Goodsel Jacobs; Ripley B. Mead, Jr.; Anthony Quarles; the late Bert Williams; seated left to right are James Summerower; Chester Dixon; Albert Johnson, and John Edelen.

Ballroom to capacity with more than 700 people for my installation banquet.

At last I had gained the attention of both the white and Black press in Chicago. As head of the Dearborn Real Estate Board I would be heard at the highest levels of government whenever I spoke out against Jim Crow practices in the housing and insurance industries.

"Quarantine the niggers" was a gentlemen's agreement within the insurance industry that had become 95% effective by the late 1950s. Black people who lived on the South and West Sides of Chicago were red-lined by 285 of the 310 casualty and fire insurance companies operating in Illinois. Insurance policies held by residents in the red-lined areas were cancelled.

Prominence in the Black community and professional standing provided no immunity from discrimination by the insurance industry. Among my clients who were affected by the mass cancellations were Earl B. Dickerson, president of Supreme Liberty Life Insurance Company; Dr. N.O. Calloway, president of the Chicago Urban League and also president of the Chicago Medical Association; Kit Baldwin, president of Baldwin Ice Cream Company; and Irving Mollison, who later was appointed U.S. Claims Court judge in New York.

The underwriting practices that permitted

insurance companies to cancel or reject policies based upon the color of one's skin rather than on an analysis of the individual financial risk made me furious. As a young businessman, I fought on the side of my neighbors rather than adopt the "go along and get along" attitude that afflicted many of my colleagues. My stand-up posture did not enhance my business with Blacks or endear me with the white insurance establishment. The only compensation I received was the ability to look in the mirror each morning while shaving a face that reflected satisfaction from doing the right thing.

My leadership of the Dearborn Real Estate Board was best described in a book entitled "Negro Politics: The Search for Leadership" by Dr. James Q. Wilson, professor of government at Harvard University:

"Dempsey J. Travis, a real estate broker, is a young and energetic businessman who has sought to organize Negro real estate and insurance men into a campaign to alter a policy of fire insurance companies that results in an inability to insure properties in Negro areas against fire losses. His energy has carried him to the presidency of the Dearborn Real Estate Board, a professional association of Negro real estate brokers and to the vice-presidency of the Chicago Insurance Brokers Association, a group of Negro insurance men. Efforts by Negroes to halt and reverse the series of fire insurance cancellations on the South Side of the city brought Travis to the forefront as an organizer and spokesman. The stake of the Negro businessmen in the issue was clearly a tangible one, since property and insurance sales are severely hampered by this inability to obtain fire coverage at a figure near the manual rates charged white buyers of insurance . . . . Travis, with a few others, held a series of meetings among interested parties in the Negro community, and then met in conference with Mayor Richard J. Daley and the state director of insurance. The meeting was also attended by major insurance company representatives. The issue was quickly seen by Negro leaders such as Travis as a racial one, and he alleged in a newspaper interview that, '290 insurance companies are practicing Jim Crow' ."

I ran unopposed for a second term as president of the board in 1958. In 1970, when I was drafted to serve a third term, I became the first person in the board's 61-year history other than the founder and first president, the late Elmore Baker, to serve as DREB president for more than two years.

Nearly 4,000 supporters attended the West Side evening rally of the Chicago Conventions Movement held at Stone Temple Baptist Church on Sunday, July 24, 1960. Pictured are Dr. Martin Luther King Jr., and Dempsey J. Travis, general coordinator of the Chicago March Committee. This picture was taken moments after Mr. Travis had introduced Dr. King to the jam packed church.

12

CHAPTER

The Civil Rights Lines North of Mason-Dixon

The Chicago branch of the NAACP was on the front line of the civil rights struggle. The Windy City chapter had more than 50,000 dues-paying members in 1959, the largest local in the country. The presidency of the Chicago chapter was a highly coveted office that bestowed on its occupant a great deal of prestige and awesome responsibilities.

To successfully lead a professional or civil rights organization requires personal commitment and financial sacrifice. Sacrifice was what some members of the Chicago Chapter of the NAACP asked of me when they urged me to run for office in the fall of 1959.

I initially refused the offer because I felt I could not afford to neglect my fledgling business. Besides, I had assumed additional responsibilities in August 1959, when I was elected first vice president of the National Association of Real Estate Brokers.

I had been the president of the Dearborn Real Estate Board two years before I met Dr. Martin Luther King Jr. and Daisey Bates. Mrs. Bates was the pillar behind her late husband, L.C. Bates, who had been the key leader in the 1957 desegregation battle at Central High School in Little Rock, Arkansas.

The sacrifice that I was being asked to consider by the officers of the NAACP was minuscule compared with the commitment that Dr. King and Mrs. Bates made when they agreed to lay their lives on the line every day in the pursuit of civil rights. Therefore it was in that frame of reference that I agreed to run for president of the local NAACP.

Gerald Bullock, a Dunbar High School teacher and civil rights organizer, was my formidable opponent. The contest was hard-fought and very political. On the night of the election in December, 1959, the Dunbar school auditorium was packed with 3,400 delegates, Blacks and whites, and 2,000 more delegates waited outside. Ballots were cast after nominating speeches were made. I will never forget the "Silk Stocking Candidate" label that the late State Rep. William Robinson hung on me in his powerful address on behalf of Mr. Bullock.

The ballots were hand-counted, and the process took all night. It was late in the morning the following day that I learned I had been elected president of the most powerful NAACP branch in the country.

Victory provided me with a broader base from which to raise my voice against insurance Jim Crowism and real estate racism. I addressed hearings before the state Senate Committee, the state House Insurance Committee and stormed the offices of Chicago Mayor Richard J. Daley and of Joseph S. Gerber, the Illinois Insurance director.

In the battle with the insurance giants I sometimes felt like a lonely voice crying in the wilderness. The struggle taught me that if you cry long enough, the tears will wash away the clouds over your eyes and you will see clearly that the solution is not in crying but in fighting back.

Never in my memory had a Chicago Black social club responded to a crisis as generously as did the Winsomettes. Their president, Bernadine Washington, presented a check to the Chicago branch of the NAACP in May 1960 in the sum of $3,000. On June 17, our NAACP held its most successful Freedom Fund Dinner, netting $31,000.

Thurgood Marshall, NAACP chief legal counsel who on Oct. 2, 1967, was sworn in as the first Black U.S. Supreme Court Justice, was the speaker at the

May, 1960: Presentation to Sammy Davis, Jr. at Winnsomets NAACP Fund Raising Affair at the old Chicago Sheraton Hotel. Left to right are Harry James, band leader; Dempsey J. Travis, Sammy Davis, Jr. and Daddy-o-Daylie.

June 1960 NAACP dinner. Marshall told the audience, which included Mayor Daley, "If we are going to fight segregation in housing in Georgia, we are going to fight it in Chicago."

The fight for freedom in Chicago was given a big boost when we received the following telegram from two of America's foremost civil rights leaders:

```
┌─────────────────────────────────────────────────────────────┐
│  ┃┃ ┃┃                                       Telegram         │
│  western union                                                │
├─────────────────────────────────────────────────────────────┤
│  LLCQ15 SA001                                                 │
│  S NNY049 NNZ48 LONG BOOK NYZ48 NL PO UUX NEW YORK NY 10      │
│  DEMPSEY TRAVIS TRAVIS REALTY              1960 JULY 11 AM 12 2S│
│  414 EAST 47 ST CHCO                                           │
│  WE ARE REQUESTING YOUR COOPERATION IN AN IMPORTANT UNDERTAKING.│
│  WE BELIEVE A MIGHTY VOICE MUST BE HEARD AT FORTHCOMING POLITICAL│
│  CONVENTIONS DEMANDING ELEMENTARY JUSTICE FOR THE NEGRO. WE    │
│  PLAN TO COME TO CONVENTION AND NEED YOUR HELP. EACH PARTY MUST│
│  REPUDIATE SEGREGATIONISTS WITHIN ITS RANKS. CHICAGO HAS HISTORICAL│
│  OPPORTUNITY TO UNIQUE CONTRIBUTION TO CIVIL RIGHTS. COURAGEOUS│
│  SOUTHERN STUDENTS AND MILLIONS OF DISFRANCHISED NEGROES LOOK  │
│  TO PEOPLE OF YOUR CITY TO REPRESENT THEM BEFORE CONVENTION.   │
│  WE URGE YOU AND OTHER COMMUNITY LEADERS TO COOPERATE WITH US, │
│  IN ORGANIZATION OF NON-VIOLENT "MARCH ON THE CONVENTIONS MOVEMENT│
│  FOR FREEDOM NOW." LOS ANGELES LEADERS BEING CALLED UPON FOR   │
│  SIMILAR ACTION. JOAN SUALT, HUNTER ODELL, AND NORMAN HILL IN  │
│  CHICAGO AS OUR REPRESENTATIVES TO ASSIST YOU IN CONVENING COMMUNITY│
│  COMMITTEE TO IMPLEMENT OUR SHARED OBJECTIVES. PLEASE WIRE READINESS│
│  TO SERVE ON COMMITTEE TO COOPERATE WITH US AND REPRESENTATIVES│
│  IN ACHIEVING OBJECTIVES OF THIS PROJECT                       │
│     A PHILIP RANDOLPH & MARTIN LUTHER KING JR 312 WEST 125TH   │
│  ST NEW YORK 27 NY.                                            │
└─────────────────────────────────────────────────────────────┘
```

The initial meeting of the Chicago March on Conventions Committee assembled in the Blue Room of the Parkway Ballroom on June 21, 1960. Bayard Rustin, who was executive assistant to A. Phillip Randolph, presided and introduced Mr. Randolph, often called the Father of the Modern Civil Rights March, addressed the purpose and the program of the March on Conventions Movement for Freedom Now.

"This demonstration shall be a protest against the conspiracy of silence on civil rights and the piecemealness which characterizes both the Republican and Democratic parties," he said.

A. Phillip Randolph, the master civil rights strategist and former leader of the Brotherhood of Sleeping Car Porters.

Randolph, who had been labeled the most dangerous man in America by President Woodrow Wilson, said the march would emphasize the need for an executive order to implement court decisions on ending segregation in housing and on guaranteeing of the right to vote. He urged us to leave no doubt that Black people in Chicago stood firmly behind leaders in the labor and liberal movements in their demand for an end to equivocation on the civil rights question.

Rustin, Randolph's heir apparent and the architect of the March on Washington that attracted more than 200,000 demonstrators August 28, 1963, emphasized the importance of a large turnout for the Chicago rally. The Los Angeles committee was planning for 5,000 to 10,000 demonstrators, and we were urged to set equally high goals. Black leadership could not be perceived as endorsing a particular political party.

"The March on Conventions Movement is a demonstration against the do-nothingness of <u>both</u> parties," said Rustin.

During the question and answer period, Randolph, with characteristic quiet dignity, welcomed and solicited the cooperation of Black Republicans in Chicago, especially those who would be delegates to the Republican National Convention. As to future plans by the movement, Randolph said, "We will cross that bridge when we get to it."

The 24 co-chairmen of the Chicago Organizing Committee elected at the meeting represented a

cross-section of organizations in the city. In a deep, baritone voice cultivated during many years of orating on the street corners of Harlem, Randolph urged the selection of a coordinator to centralize the responsibility for the march. The titles of convenor and general march coordinator fell to me by unanimous consent.

Thousands of cards were printed to urge people to pledge their support and participation. A small staff comprising Timuel D. Black, Norman Hill, Bennet Johnson, Joan Sualt and Carl Fuqua, executive secretary of the Chicago branch of the NAACP, performed the Herculean task of enlisting support groups in only 17 days.

The pre-convention March for Freedom Now rally was held Sunday, July 24, 1960. Some 5,000 supporters heard remarks by Roy Wilkins, New York Gov. Nelson A. Rockefeller and A. Phillip Randolph. The nearly 4,000 supporters who attended the evening rally held at Stone Temple Baptist Church were addressed by Dr. King and Mr. Randolph.

At 4 p.m., July 25, 1960, demonstrators assembled in front of Rev. Louis Rawls' Tabernacle Baptist Church. At 5:10 p.m. more than 10,000 marchers, by a police count, stepped off proudly enroute to the Amphitheatre at Root and Halsted, the site of the G.O.P. convention.

The Chicago march was the largest demonstration of its kind held in the country. Sharing the front line were Dr. King, Randolph, Rev. Ralph Abernathy and Travis. Right behind us were the student sit-in leaders: Diane Nash, Bernard Lee and Marion Barry, later mayor of Washington, D.C. We marched north on Indiana and west on 39th Street singing to the tune of "I've Been Working on the Railroad:"

"We've been marching on the vigil
All the live long day.
And we'll be marching on the vigil
Till Americans change their ways.
Can't you hear our plea for freedom?
Rise up so early in the morn.
Can't you hear our plea for freedom?
Put Civil Rights in your platform!"

That fine hour faded quickly.

In 1960, civil rights in Chicago had barely crawled out of the Dark Ages. White teenage hoodlums harassed Black youths in the schools and on the streets.

Private business schools in the Loop did not have a race problem, simply because they did not admit Blacks. Here is but one example: Mary L. Jackson and Rachel Hawkins, who were employed as secretaries at the Navy Pier University of Illinois Campus, were denied admission to the Moser Evening School because they were African-Americans. The reason for the action was explained by Mrs. Paul Moser, the school's president, who politely said, "We never have."

Jim Crow practices that infected American employment housing and health care extended unto the grave. A sign reading "For Caucasians Only" graced the gate of the Oakwood Cemetery on Chicago's South Side.

On the Sunday afternoon of August 29th, I was informed by a Sun-Times newspaper reporter that the NAACP Youth Council, which included 40 Blacks and 10 white sympathizers, were holding a wade-in at Rainbow Beach, between 75th and 77th Streets on the lakefront. This was a Lake Michigan beach where Blacks had been hounded by lifeguards and white bathers for many years.

The council's objective was to give Chicago an opportunity to disown its title of the most segregated city in the nation by allowing Black citizens to wade in the blue waters of the lake. But the NAACP sponsors could not prevent the violence that erupted after 21-year-old Velma Murphy was hit with a rock. White youths, some armed with stones in the presence of 96 policemen, followed the autos of the demonstrators west to Stony Island Avenue.

Although objectives had not been completed by the end of my term as NAACP president, I declined to run for re-election. I had been truant from Travis Realty Company, Sivart Mortgage Corporation and the Travis Insurance Agency for three years, and regretfully concluded that a longer absence might result in surrendering my business to an early grave.

Unattended businesses generally go into a holding pattern before they fold up and disappear. Black businesses often instantly self-destruct. My business had neither self-destructed nor disappeared, but it was fading fast. Sales volume at Travis Realty for 1960 dropped 40 percent from the previous year. Sivart did not receive an authorization from the Federal Housing Administration to act as mortgage loan correspondent for the Chicago Metropolitan Mutual Assurance Company until August 1, 1960. This meant few, if any, FHA loans could be generated and closed before January 1, 1961.

Our insurance sales suffered the same results as the real estate sales. The price I paid for vigorous involvement with civil rights came within a hairline of destroying my career.

The white establishments called me a demagogue. Black business peers privately called me a fool, a fool for investing my time in what they considered unrelenting and unsolvable Black problems.

Looking back over the past 30 years, I am convinced that my participation in the civil rights movement is possibly the best investment I could ever make. There is no higher calling than working for the betterment of human welfare. Therefore I have no regret for taking the road that was riddled with potholes and open sewers.

Presentation of the first "Black Enterprise Magazine Award In Finance" by Vice President Nelson A. Rockefeller to Dempsey J. Travis and Mrs. Travis at the White House, February 21, 1975.

13

CHAPTER

A Housing Revolution Without Bloodshed

At the dawn of the 1960s, President John Fitzgerald Kennedy turned on the lights at the end of the housing corridor for Black Americans. His successor, Lyndon Baines Johnson, was a keeper of the flame. In the early 1970s, President Richard Milhouse Nixon dimmed the lights again, and they have barely flickered during the Reagan-Bush era.

The 1960s opened the gate for Black participation in the housing market, the restraints that had been imposed by both the private and the public sectors had been partially lifted. In Chicago, for instance, Black home ownership increased 100 percent in the decade between 1960 and 1970.

The tactics used to open housing for minorities had been ineffective. The Civil Rights Act of 1866, for example, stated, "All citizens of the United States shall have the same right in every state and territory, as is enjoyed by white citizens thereof, to inherit, purchase, lease, sell, hold and convey real and personal property." In 1917, the U.S. Supreme Court held racial zoning ordinances invalid (*Buchanan* v. *Warley*); the Supreme Court in 1948 ruled that racially restrictive covenants were judicially unenforceable (*Shelley* v. *Kraemer*). The Housing Act of 1949 was Congress' attempt to set a standard living environment for every American family.

Early in the 1950s, mortgage banking became the primary vehicle for channeling FHA & VA housing investment dollars from major insurance companies and pension funds into the white housing market. Between 1947 and 1960 the government insured more than 1 million mortgage loans for veterans in suburban areas and 800,000 for veterans in the cities; 99.5% of the mortgage loans approved north of the Mason-Dixon line were for white veterans. The pittance of VA and FHA loans made to urban Blacks were byproducts of a campaign initiated in 1953 by the National Association of Real Estate Brokers (NAREB), the Black counterpart to the National Association of Real Estate Boards.

NAREB's campaign, abetted by local groups

such as the Dearborn Real Estate Board, effected a compromise. The deal was the incorporation of the Voluntary Home Mortgage Credit Program (VHMCP) into the Housing Act of 1954 which was the first federal recognition that minority citizens needed affirmative action to obtain home financing.

President Dwight David Eisenhower brought attention to the VHMCP in his State of the Union message on January 24, 1954 when he said: "Many members of minority groups, regardless of their income or economic status, have had the least opportunity of all citizens to acquire good homes." But the VHMCP was merely a re-enactment of the fox guarding the chicken house. The racist lenders who had denied Blacks loans through the conventional financing sources ran the VHMCP. Travis Realty Company dropped out of the program.

The disastrous direction taken by the VHMCP was pivotal in my decision to organize Sivart Mortgage Company to circumvent the Cotton Curtain in the mortgage market. That proved difficult because the Federal Housing Administration would not approve an application for an African American to become a certified mortgage banker in 1954. The first application for a Black mortgage banker was approved eight years later when the Democrats regained the White House.

There were no Black mortgage bankers when

President John F. Kennedy took office. His appointment of Robert C. Weaver, an African American, as
administrator of the Housing and Home Finance
Agency was a strong signal that democracy in housing was on the march from the Oval Office to the
poorer neighborhoods around the country whence
people of color might find the assistance to make the
American dream of owning your own home a reality.

*Plaque presentation to Dr. Robert C. Weaver, Secretary of the U.S.
Department of Housing and Urban Development by Mr. Dempsey J.
Travis, President and Chairman of the Board, United Mortgage
Bankers of America. The ceremony was held at the Mid-Winter
Meeting of the UMBA in the Waldorf Astoria Hotel, New York City,
February 12, 1964.*

The new president meant business. The executive order he signed Nov. 20, 1962, proclaimed to the banking and real estate industries that all federal

Dempsey J. Travis, President of United Mortgage Bankers of America greets Robert Kennedy, United States Attorney General during President John F. Kennedy's Administration.

agencies must henceforth prevent discrimination based on race, creed or national origin in federally assisted housing programs.

The VA, the FHA and subsidized public housing were among the agencies and programs affected.

President Kennedy declared "It is neither proper nor equitable that Americans should be denied the benefits of housing owned by the federal government or financed through federal assistance on the basis of their race, color, creed, or national origin. Our national policy is equal opportunity for all and the Federal Government will continue to take such legal and proper steps as it may to achieve the realization of that goal."

Equal housing advocates hailed the turn-around as the beginning of a social revolution, but they were soon disappointed. The executive order changed the rhetoric of the banking establishment, but it did not change the engrained discriminatory practices.

Opponents of civil rights decried the edict, insisting it would incite riots in the streets and economic catastrophe. They were wrong.

The national mood following the housing proclamation was relatively peaceful. The housing market did not collapse and builders and lenders did not close their shops. A building boom was under way.

The FHA had received mortgage insurance applications for 282,500 new units by November 1963, including 191,700 for single-family dwellings and 90,800 for multifamily units.

On November 22, 1963, one year and two

days after his executive order introduced democracy in American housing, President Kennedy was assassinated in Dallas, Texas.

The openness of the Kennedy and Johnson administrations was a godsend.

Access to capital is the lifeblood of any institution or organization. During my first months in the mortgage banking business, I tried to raise the Cotton Curtain alone and failed. In the fall of 1962, I organized the United Mortgage Bankers of America because Blacks were locked out of the "Lilly white" Mortgage Bankers Association of America and its subsidiaries.

UMBA conducted extensive regional and national surveys that confirmed the uniform lockout of Blacks from the mortgage market. We spoke before church and civic organizations throughout the nation. Our other civil rights strategies ranged from picketing the giant size insurance companies and boycotting national major lenders. The tactics got their attention and ultimately paid off.

In February 1963, a $10 million dollar mortgage commitment was made to three of UMBA's member companies by the International Ladies Garment Workers Union, headquartered in New York City. Prior to this breakthrough, the sole source of funds for Black mortgage bankers was from small Black life insurance companies.

A total of 50 million dollars in mortgage money made available during calendar year 1963 was via banks and savings and loan associations based in New York City. The success was the result of 40 Black mortgage bankers from across the face of America working together to achieve a single objective: to open the mortgage market to Black Americans. The UMBA members worked in teams of four and made personal calls on 63 banks, 48 life insurance companies and 10 savings and loan associations before the money was released.

UMBA's strategy was described by its first president, Dempsey J. Travis, as "quiet persuasion". The group urged white-owned financial institutions to consider these facts: 85 percent of the savings of Black Americans were in major white financial institutions; 38 percent of African American families, compared with 62 percent of white families, were homeowners. The number of Black households with an annual income of more than $5,000 rose almost 20-fold between 1950 and 1960: from 43,000 to 766,000. The majority of these families were forced to live in substandard dwellings although they could afford reasonably priced houses.

The minority housing market was further stimulated in 1969 when the insurance industry launched an unprecedented $2 billion urban investment program at the urging of President Richard M.

Officers, directors, and charter members of the United Mortgage Bankers of America. Picture was taken February 18, 1963, at the Americana Hotel in New York City during the first Mid-Winter Meeting of UMBA. Seated, left to right are: J.W. Robinson, senior vice president, Houston, Texas; Dempsey J. Travis, president and chairman of the board, Chicago, Illinois; Joseph T. Bickers, secretary, Atlanta, Georgia; and Robert L. Hughes, assistant secretary, Kansas City, Missouri. Standing, left to right are: James Lynch, Chicago, Illinois; M. J. Anderson, Austin Texas; G.W. Gates, St. Louis, Missouri; C.W. Calloway, Atlanta Georgia; George Haley, Kansas City, Missouri; Millard Robbins, Chicago, Illinois; George W. Crank, General Counsel, Chicago, Illinois; Jesse Johnson, Jr., Denver, Colorado, and Q.V. Williamson, Atlanta, Georgia.

Nixon. In tandem with the President's program, FHA announced its intention to insure single-family mortgages in previously redlined minority areas.

UMBA had at last achieved what its detractors had predicted was "a wild dream" seven years earlier. But the dream had not been completely realized. African Americans were denied the education that could prepare them for careers in finance. Enrollment in mortgage banking schools was restricted to members of the white trade associations.

My situation was perhaps typical. The only academic exposure to mortgage banking I had received before organizing the Sivart Mortgage Corporation had been gleaned from reading the financial pages of the newspapers and real estate trade magazines.

My obsession with obtaining a viable education was not so typical. Denied access to the courses I needed, I took a bold step in the spring of 1965 and wrote President Lyndon Baines Johnson and requested that he intercede in my behalf to gain membership in the Mortgage Bankers of America. The president assigned the White House counsel to investigate my allegation. After an exchange of letters and telephone calls between the White House and the MBA headquarters, which was located at 111 West Washington in Chicago, I received a membership application in the late fall of 1965.

The application required two active MBA members as signatories. I visited a dozen mortgage banking officials in downtown Chicago and each one offered some off the wall reason for not signing on. Finally, I arranged to meet with the president of one of the largest mortgage banking firms in the industry. During our meeting, I told him that the president of the United States was interested in seeing my MBA application processed, his response was startling: "To hell with the president," he blurted. I left his office and walked slowly into the shadows of the LaSalle Street canyons wondering if the whole damned world were anti-Black.

Just as I was about to give up, I remembered meeting Harry Gottlieb, a mortgage banker, at some civic function. I turned around in the middle of the crowded sidewalk and went directly to his office in the Inland Steel Building on West Monroe.

Harry looked at the application and then at me, and said, "You are a red hot number, Travis. If you were white I would automatically sign this application, so I am not going to let the fact that you are Black change my behavior."

Harry noted that I banked at Central National Bank and suggested that Marvin Reynolds, a senior vice president at that institution, should be the second signatory, Reynolds complied, and my application was approved.

*Pictured in this 1968 photo are: Vice President Hubert H. Humphrey,
and Dempsey J. Travis. This photo was taken in July at the Blackstone
Hotel, Chicago.*

With that hurdle out of the way, I was inves-
tigated by the MBA membership committee as if I
was going to be appointed an Associate Justice of the
United States Supreme Court. Being cleared of
whatever they were looking for, I was admitted to
the School of Mortgage Banking at Northwestern
University in the summer of 1966. I graduated (the
lone Black mortgage banker) in the class of '69.

The appointment of nine African Americans and one Spanish-speaking mortgage correspondent by the Federal National Mortgage Association (FNMA) in 1969 gave a big thrust to the Black mortgage banking industry. But, national priorities shifted and the alliance between HUD and the insurance industry faded during the second year of the Nixon administrations. Although the nation was still sorely in need of low- and moderately priced housing, President Nixon focused his commitments toward Black capitalism.

When Nixon took office in 1969, there were five Black mortgage banking companies in Chicago and 50 across the nation. By 1981, Sivart Mortgage was the only one left in Chicago, and the number nationwide had dropped to seven.

The Sivart mortgage banking presence in Chicago not only raised the Cotton Curtain between the Black community and the Federal Housing Administration. It also created jobs for African Americans in companies that had never considered hiring a Black employee or accepting a mortgage application from a minority applicant.

John Kennedy's New Frontier and Lyndon Johnson's Great Society set the stage and made it possible for UMBA to lift the Cotton Curtain and open up some real economic opportunities in a once lilly-white industry.

President Jimmy Carter and Dempsey J. Travis in the East Room of the White House, Washington, D.C., December 20, 1979 following briefing and luncheon meeting.

CHAPTER

Dreaming Poor And Thinking Poor Are The Wrong Roads to Success

When I was growing up, our family had breakfast together only one day a week, and that was on Sundays. On the other six days, my father had to leave for work shortly after 5 a.m.

One Sunday Dad had his head buried in the sports section of the Chicago Tribune and was oblivious to the excitement in my voice when I said, "I dreamed last night that I was going to be rich and Daddy wouldn't have to get up before daylight to go to work anymore. I was 6 years old and had not been fed any "dream food", which was what we called dishes laden with fatback.

Mother awarded my fantasies with a warm smile. My father folded his paper abruptly and looked at me.

"Everybody wants to be rich, boy," he said. "You concentrate on getting that food into your mouth and then worry about how you're going to get through this day without getting a spanking."

"That was a true dream," I said. "That dream was as clear as the day is long, Daddy. I figure it's just a matter of working hard."

"Your mother and I, and your uncles, don't know nothing but hard work," he scoffed.

I took a few more bites out of my apple. "I understand that," I said. "It's just — well, if a person really sets out to be rich, you know, and plan and work at it, well, it might happen outside of a dream. Mr. Charles Murray across the street is rich. Why not me?"

Dad smiled, shook his head, and before picking up his paper, retorted: "Okay, millionaire, it sounds as easy as apple pie, but maybe your dream might come true." He then patted me on my head thinking it was packed with delusions.

Years later, as I scoured the city in search of get-rich plans, I often received that kind of bemused look that Columbus must have witnessed when he insisted that the world was round. In search of my own new world, I refused to be discouraged by the prevailing belief that a Black man's chances of making it big in the world of commerce were razor thin.

Admittedly, I was a naive child. As a young adult I still couldn't abandon the idea that Black-controlled business was not the way to bring more African Americans into mainstream America. The deeper I delved into the history of the early Black entrepreneurs, the more convinced I became that I was on the right track.

It seemed only fair play that Blacks ride atop the wagons of commerce that they had pulled without compensation for 300 years.

I first entered the business world to provide a comfortable living for my family, and in the glow of my success have not been lured into the lavish lifestyle that many of my friends have adopted.

One reason I am an alien in the world of the rich and the famous is that I draw my fulfillment from a deeper well. My success flies in the face of those who out of the reach of my ear predicted I would never make it. Successful Black American entreprenueurs are hung in effigy daily by Black skeptics and white racists.

My attitude toward material success is entertwined with my perceptions of the political and economic state of African Americans. Early in my career — when my success was still pretty shaky — I became involved in civil rights projects that were detrimental to my business activities because controversial stands were contrary to the rules of the establishment. I was constantly rocking the "Old Boys" ship.

I discovered early on that people who go out of their way to empathize with the brothers and sisters who have no bootstraps can look in the mirror every morning and say: "I am giving my best." When you can honestly make that statement your personal success will become important to thousands of people you may never meet. And I have been rewarded many times by some stranger who has stopped me on the street to thank me for some public statement or action that he or she thought was on the mark.

It is true that some of the "have nots" will interpret your empathy as weakness and your social concern as naivete. But you can usually count on your God-given barracuda instincts to balance the scale when it becomes necessary to protect your back.

Business success requires a single-mindedness. Your commercial goals must be in the forefront of your mind. This requires a discipline that costs more in personal sacrifice than most people are either willing or able to make. The aura of success is sweet, but the price is never cheap.

The real achievers I know are not clock-watchers. Dillettants who become obsessed with "party time" seldom survive in a business climate because they are too busy performing a rehashed dance that a decade ago we called the "Madison" and is now

Pictured are Donald Walker and the Rev. Jesse Jackson making presentation of first "Black Businessman of the Year" award to Dempsey J. Travis. Photo taken Dec. 3, 1970.

known as the "Electric Slide". While they are sliding, the clock of commerce is ticking away. Social experiments can go on forever, but a viable business plan is finite. There is no lay away plan for holding back the hands of time.

Time is a tool that must be carefully used. My methods for training our marketing people about the principle of time were not always orthodox. At the beginning of each sales meeting in the early days of my real estate firm, I would have one of the salesmen read aloud the obituary of some prominent citizens that appeared in the morning paper. This was an attempt to cure the salesmen of procrastination, a disease that they all suffered from to some degree. The "I will do it tomorrow or next week" virus is contagious, and my daily reading of the obituary columns still reminds me that the time to act is now. In my travels around the country I've found that the most comprehensive obituaries appear in the New York Times. A good obit can offer some good clues on how "Old Joe" made his millions.

I try to invest my time the same way I invest my money. I spend very little on small talk or small thoughts. My efforts are designed to yield an uninterrupted flow of intellectual and monetary benefits. On lucky days, they yield both.

A projected timetable is important to any economic plan. You never stretch four hours of work into an eight-hour time frame. Many business managers know former employees who have taken a two hour task and made it an eight hour project. Permitting that to happen is going out of business through the back door.

These strategies will yield dividends for anyone, Black or white. But Blacks face some special hurdles if they want success. One is genuine fear of risk, which I do not discount. Many of our fears are realistic, but I believe we too frequently surrender to imaginary phobias. We opt for security over risk without really exploring our own full capabilities.

My mother and my wife believed that if I took a nice job at the post office we would be assured of a paycheck twice a month and have economic security for life. They had my best interests at heart, but they discounted my abilities. They thought the world was going to prove too much for me. If I had lowered my aspirations to match theirs, today I'd probably be one of the best retired letter sorters in Chicago! I would also have missed the exhilarating roller coaster of business life where you experience a chill with every drop in the market and a thrill with every climb.

Many young educated Blacks attempting to secure their niche in corporate America discover that they are in a trap and become paralyzed by their anger and frustration, unable to act until they are kicked out of the door. Education and on-the-job training is not enough if you don't have enough street smarts to recognize that entrepreneurship may be a Black person's only escape hatch to personal freedom.

I have felt the rage that overpowers many African Americans, but I never permitted it to overwhelm me. Rage is self-destructive. It is foolhardy to program ourselves to hate Caucasians or any other ethnic group. Hate destroys the hater while the hated continue to ring the cash registers.

Reading and an ongoing education program are top prerequisites for operating a successful business. During my first 20 years in real estate, I carried at least 10 academic hours in evening courses each year and read 10 newspapers every day: the five Chicago papers, plus the Wall Street Journal, American Banker, The Washington Post, The New York Times and the Christian Science Monitor. My current literary diet includes reading at least six newspapers a day plus four books and a dozen trade journals a month.

Academic training, combined with experience, taught me how to look at an almost devastated piece of real estate and see a gold mine instead of a disaster. The first lesson I learned was never to buy other people's paint. I've saved as much as 300 percent by repairing the "old girl" myself instead of paying a much higher price for a painted doll.

Rising early is a common trait among all the successful people I've known. I've always had a high energy level, which is a product of genetics and lifestyle, and long ago stopped worrying about being different. My friends, many of whom are deceased, frequently told me to slow down. My inevitable

Dempsey J. Travis is seated at the head of the table at this session of the Presidential Task Force on Urban Renewal. Picture taken at the White House, 1970.

response would be to ask why they didn't speed up because time and tide waits for no man - or woman.

These attributes have paid off literally in more honors than I could have evered imagine: President Johnson asked me to participate in the White House Conference, To Fulfill These Rights, in 1966. President Nixon appointed me to the task force that drafted the 1970 Housing Bill. President Ford appointed me to a think tank task force on energy and inflation. Vice President Nelson Rockefeller presented me with the first Black Enterprise Magazine Award in finance at the White House in 1975; I accepted President Jimmy Carter's invitation to a White House briefing and luncheon in the fall of 1979.

When I shared the dais with presidential candidate Ronald Reagan at the Executive Club of Chicago in 1979, few members or guests believed he would make it to the White House. To most of them he was just an out-of-work actor and too old to be elected. Reagan astonished his detractors because he refused to learn to fail.

African Americans are in a unique situation: we spend so much energy fighting nightmares that very little is left for our dreams. Of course, conditions can be downright sickening at times. But we must not forget that with all our handicaps and entrapments, Blacks increased their annual national income from $50 billion in 1960 to $127 billion in 1980. There were more than 1 million Blacks attending college in 1980, compared with a quarter of a million in 1966. A multitude of Black public officials have been elected throughout the land, including mayors in large major cities such as Chicago, Atlanta, New Orleans, Detroit, Kansas City, Mo., Los Angeles, Denver, Hartford, Newark, Cleveland, Gary, New York City, and Washington, D.C.

The first Black president of the United States has already been born and will be elected before the year 2010, providing the rest of us build on the legal victories of the 1940s and 1950s, the civil rights struggles of the 1960s and the political victories of the 1970s and 80s.

When I was 38, many of my friends thought the high point of my career had been reached with my election to a second term as president of the Dearborn Real Estate Board. They knew how important that was to me, and to the Black business community, and assumed I'd be taking things a little easier after reaching that summit.

One of those friends was the late Wilbur Slaughter, a fellow realtist. He was a very astute copper-colored, gaunt-faced man. One late afternoon before a board meeting he looked me dead in the eye and said, "Boy are you lucky! This has got to be the zenith of your real estate career."

I smiled and said to myself, "Man, are you wrong. This is nice, sure. But there is going to be a lot more to my life than this."

And there was.

And there are more chapters to come.

"Man, I'm sorry, but I just remembered ----- you not s'posed to sleep on white sheets, you s'posed to have blue sheets!"

Epilogue

The Chicago of my yesteryears was 100 percent Black after sundown when the white landlords and merchants closed their offices and shops and went home to the suburbs.

The late Chicago Mayor Harold Washington crystallized the period between 1920 and 1942: "I went through the same Jim Crow nonsense that most Black people experienced in Chicago. I lived in an incubator. The South Side was my world. I would get on my bike and ride all over the entire South Side and not come in personal contact with a single white person."

In those years, the best and the brightest African Americans lived within a stone's throw of people who by 1990s standards would be classified as the underclass. Proximity to the middle-class Blacks provided a wide window of opportunity from which to watch and learn.

Some of the most powerful and successful of today's African Americans were yesterday's urchins. Their springboard from the streets to the suites came through observing or adopting as mentors, even vicariously, the Black achievers who lived next door, down the block, across the street or around the corner.

Although restrictive housing covenants, rather than individual preferences, defined where African Americans could live until 1948, the mobility of successful Blacks during the past three decades has created a void in leadership for those who stay in the old neighborhoods. There are few role models left to meet urban youth on the streets of their own communities and encourage them to stay in school and study hard so that they, too, can achieve financial security through legitimate avenues.

Role models in the 1990s spring not from the neighborhood, but from TV and movie screens. Young people watching "In Living Color" see Willie, the coke dealer, looking cool as he drives a Jeep Grand Wagoneer around the school. They identify with Baby Wimp the Pimp, who rides through the streets in his Mercedes Benz 560 SEL to monitor his girls. Who among their elders point out that the real role model on that TV show is Keenen Ivory Wayans, whose comedic talents and fiscal savvy are founded in self-discipline, determination and dedication?

Many big-money athletes live in white suburbs or in some sections of a city where they are oddities rather than role models. The Black idols jumped ship early, taking their talents, and investment capital away from communities that needed them both. They focus their future on the suburbs in spite of overwhelming evidence that the central urban areas will be the new frontiers of the 21st century.

Chicago Planning Commissioner Charles Thurow announced plans in September 1991 for the first phase of a $3 billion, 72 acre neighborhood development on the Near South Side, the second-largest in Chicago history. Black gladiators are missing out on investment opportunities like these, in part because many of their white agents advise them to live and invest in more affluent and currently "acceptable" white communities.

Chicago Bulls home games are played in a stadium on the Near West Side near hundreds of acres that have laid dormant since the riots of 1968. The twist is a Black entertainment mogul, and not a sports star, has carved out a permanent financial presence in that community.

I arrived at this fact in late 1991 when I made a windshield appraisal of the exterior of Oprah Winfrey's Harpo Studios, Inc., which occupies a square city block on the Near West Side. Although I am not privy to Ms. Winfrey's investment plans, there is no doubt in my mind that her choice of location was a deliberate and very astute business decision.

Ms. Winfrey's entrepreneurial accomplishments and sensitivity have placed her in a class beyond category. She is to America in the last decade of the 20th century what Madame C.J. Walker was in the first decade of the 1900s. Madame Walker, a cosmetics manufacturer, was one of the first American women of any race to become a millionaire independent of inheritance. Like Madame Walker, multimillionaire Winfrey saw some old bricks and proceeded to mold them into a castle from which she and her multiracial staff produce first-rate entertainment.

The new Comiskey Park is an example of restoring a historic neighborhood -in this case, a Black community on the Near South Side where Scott Joplin lived in 1900. The White Sox players cannot reach their park without passing through the area. How many of the Black kings of swat have let down their buckets in the tradition of Booker T. Washington.

Some white-complexioned brothers and sisters return to their roots, and honor ours, with financial assistance. Julius Rosenwald was a role model of social responsibility. When the financier died in 1932, more than one-fourth of all African American school children were attending classes in buildings whose construction was subsidized by the philanthropist.

Now men and women from Clifton Place in Brooklyn, N.Y. long for a home on Long Island or dare to dream of living in Westchester County, N.Y. Parents who watch youngsters deal drugs around East 12th and Chicon streets in Austin, Texas would like to move a few blocks away, around Old Fort Hill Road, where Black professionals rear their children in comfort. Houstonites from the Third and Fifth wards flock to Sharpstown and Missouri City, Texas as soon as they can rub two quarters together. Black residents in Los Angeles' Crenshaw district float to Harbor City or View Park, Calif. New Jerseyites escape from Clinton Avenue in Trenton to the suburban safety of Ewing.

Buppies flee the Black community faster than rabbits run from a forest fire. The generation whose slogan is "I Got Mine" is too busy to be reminded they owe a lifetime tax to the thousands of Black and white Americans who bled and died in the mud holes of the South and mean streets of the North. The neo-establishment Negro is blind to the sacrifices that made it possible for them to cross over into Buppieland.

Clarence Thomas, Thomas Sowell, Stanley Crouch, Shelby Steele and other Black conservatives in ivory towers may philosophize about the plight of African Americans, but they cannot understand and empathize with the less fortunate citizens who must look like aliens from another planet when they are viewed from the prism of prejudice.

The stains of racism have been woven deeply into our national fabric. Had the impurities of racism been implanted or stamped, there might be an outside chance that they could be washed away by the tides of justice.

Bibliography

BOOKS

Adams, Russell L., *Great Negroes: Past and Present*, Chicago: Afro-Am Publishing Co., 1963.

Frazier, E. Franklin, *The Negro Family in the United States*, revised and abridged, Chicago: University of Chicago Press, 1966.

Johnson, John H. with Lerone Bennett Jr., *Succeeding Against the Odds*, New York: Warner Books, 1989.

Killens, John Oliver, *And Then We Heard The Thunder*, Alfred A. Knoph, New York, 1962.

Lee, Ulysses, *United States Army and World War II: Special Studies: The Employment of Negro Troops*, Washington, D.C.: Office of the Chief of Military History United States Army, 1966.

Rather, Ernest R., Editor, *Chicago Negro Almanac and Reference Book*, Chicago: Chicago Negro Almanac Publishing Co., 1972.

Schoenfeld, Seymour J., *The Negro In the Armed Forces: His Value and Status, Past, Presently, and Potential*, Washington D.C., The Associated Publishers, 1945.

Terkel, Studs, *The Good War: An Oral History of World War II*, New York: Pantheon Books Inc., 1984.

Travis, Dempsey J., *Don't Stop Me Now*, Chicago: Children's Press, 1970.

Travis, Dempsey J., *Harold: The People's Mayor*, Chicago: Urban Research Press, Inc., 1989.

Travis, Dempsey J., *An Autobiography of Black Chicago*, Chicago: Urban Research Press, Inc., 1981.

Travis, Dempsey J., *An Autobiography of Black Politics*, Chicago: Urban Research Press, Inc., 1987.

Travis, Dempsey J., *Racism: American Style, A Corporate Gift*, Chicago: Urban Research Press, Inc., 1991.

Wilson, James Q., *Negro Politics: The Search for Leadership*, Glencoe, IL: The Free Press, 1960.

NEWSPAPER ARTICLES

"Reign of Terror Against Black Soldiers in Valle Jo, California," *Chicago Daily Defender*, 2 January 1943.

"Flag raised at Shenango personnel replacement depot as officers begin duties.Workers push building of post as men arrive." *Youngstown, Ohio Vindicator*, 10 January 1943.

"Segregation Rules WAAC Race Volunteers Lag," by Enoch P. Waters, Jr., *Chicago Daily Defender*, 16 January 1943.

"Pennsylvania Railroad ends Jim Crow Trains in State of Illinois," *Chicago Daily Defender*, 16 January 1943.

"Ask Street Car Jobs for Negroes," *Chicago Daily Defender*, 16 January 1943.

"Savoy Ballroom Closed; Mixed Dancers Seen Cause," by Alfred Duckett, *Chicago Daily Defender*, 1 May 1943.

"Covenant Ban Loses Test in Legislature," *Chicago Daily Defender*, 12 June 1943.

"Seven Die, 150 Hurt in Ten Outbreaks," *Chicago Daily Defender*, 19 June 1943.

"Riots at a Glance," *Chicago Daily Defender*, 26 June 1943.

"Blame Prejudice Police for Detroit Fatalities," *Chicago Daily Defender*, 26 June 1943.

"Riots in Los Angeles," *Chicago Daily Defender*, 26 June 1943.

"Race Riot Prob Pressed by Army: Board Named by Colonel Lawlon is making investigation", *Pittsburgh Gazette*, July 1943.

"Colored Soldiers open fire after stealing rifles: Personnel replacement depot officers say offenders broke locks to supply building and obtained arms after arguement at post exchange; Investigation is under way." July 1943.

"One killed, seven wounded at Shenango: Dispute between white and Negro troops results in trouble at camp."*Youngstown, Ohio Vindicator*, 12 July 1943.

"Blast Detroit Mayor in Cop Whitewash," *Chicago Daily Defender*, 17 July 1943.

"Van Dorn Soldiers Keep Arms," *Chicago Daily Defender*, 17 July 1943.

"Dr. Charles Drew Wins 29th Spingarn Medal," *Afro-American*, 1 April 1944.

"General Davis denies saying Army free of Bias," by J. Robert Smith, *Afro-American*, 15 April 1944.

"Increased Racial Tension Looms in San Francisco," *Afro-American*, 15 April 1944.

"Ask Volunteers for Ethiopia," *Afro-American*, 15 April 1944.

"Racial Progress cited at Tuskegee," 15 April 1944.

"Robeson Weeps as 8,000 Cheer at Birthday Party," 22 April 1944.

"Hitler Preaches Ghetto System, U.S. Practices it," *Afro-American,* 29 April 1944.

""CIAA Hits Army, Navy for Ignoring Colored Athletes," *Afro-American,* 29 April 1944.

"30 Get Wings at Tuskegee," *Afro-American,* 27 May 1944.

"Dancer Joins Negro USO Camp Shows Unit," *The New York Age,* 3 June 1944.

Memories of Racial Confrontation Resurrections," *Charon, PA Herald,* 27 July 1984.

"Philadelphia Scene of Riot in Protest against Negro Motormen," *The New York Age,* 5 August 1944.

"Army Accounts Downplayed Reynolds Racial Battle," *Charon, PA Herald,* 10 August 1984.

"Philadelphia Strike ended; Four strike leaders arrested, Fired from jobs; Army still on the Job," *The New York Age,* 12 August 1944.

"D.C. Rooms Advertised for 'Light Colored' Tenants," *Afro-American,* 15 August 1944.

"War Department order forbidding discrimination at Army posts is protested by Governor of Alabama," *The New York Age,* 21 September 1944.

"57 Negro Soldiers Jailed in Arizona when they strike against prolonged K.P. Duty," *The New York Age,* 23 September 1944.

"President Roosevelt approves Navy's plan to enlist Negro Women as Waves and SPARS," *The New York Age,* 28 October 1944.

"Negro and White Wainwright WAC's separated in Iowa, paper charges," *The New York Age,* November 1944.

"President Roosevelt Declares for permanent FEPC; Wants post-war period free from discrimination," *The New York Age,* 4 November 1944.

"For Black Soldiers there was one war, but two armies." *Pittsburgh Post Gazette,* 8 May 1985.

LETTERS

Letter from Levi H. Jolly, Editor-Manager, *Philadelphia Afro-American*, to.. showing Gibson, Jr, special assistant to secretary of War dept, Washington, D.C. July 21, 1942.

Letter from Walter White, secretary of the NAACP to Henry L. Stimson, secretary of War dated July 14, 1943.

Letter from Truman K. Gibson Jr., acting civilian aide to the Secretary of war to Mr. P.L. Prattis, Executive Editor, *Pittsburgh Courier* dated July 14 1943.

Letter from Levi H. Jolly, Editor-Manager, *Philadelphia Afro-American*, to Truman K. Gibson Jr., acting civilian aide requesting a list of all camps of Pennsylvania and Delaware and names of commanding officers, July 21, 1943.

Letter from Henry L. Stimson, secretary of War to Carl Murphy, editor, *Baltimore, MDAfro-American*, dated August 4, 1943.

Letter from Truman K. Gibson, Jr., acting civilian aide to the secretary of war, to Levi H. Jolly, Editor-Manager. *Philadelphia Afro-American*, dated August 12, 1943.

Letter from Truman K. Gibson, acting civilian aide to the secretary of war, to Mr. Walter White, secretary of the NAACP signed by ... dated September 4, 1943.

Letter from Henry L. Stimson, secretary of War to Walter White, secretary of the NAACP dated October 4, 1943.

Letter from Harold Johnson, reporter for *The Charon, PA Herald* to Dempsey Travis, dated August 21, 1944.

Letter from Tom Waseleski, reporter for the *Pittsburgh, PA Post-Gazette* dated May 8, 1985.

Letter from Howard Landy of Syasset, New York to Dempsey Travis dated July 15, 1988.

U.S. ARMY DOCUMENTS FROM THE NATIONAL ARCHIVES.

Confidential document from headquarters third service command, U.S. Army, Intelligence Division, 7th floor, Standard Oil Building, Baltimore, MD; Document Number 8991, referencing a letter from your office July 17, 1943. Subject: Race riot at Shenango personnel replacement depot. File SPX 2991.2   14, July, 1943 signed off by F.S. Doll, Colonel, G.S.C. director.

A letter dated August 9, 1943 to Mr. P.L. Prattis, Executive Editor, Pittsburgh Courier, Pittsburgh, PA; Re: story that appeared in July 17th issue of the Pittsburgh Courier. The letter was signed by Truman K. Gibson Jr., civilian aide to the secretary of war.

Memorandum from Truman J. Gibson, Jr. acting civilian aide to the secretary of war, to Colonel Stanley J. Grogan states in the second paragraph that stories that appear in *Afro-American* and *Pittsburgh Courier* Newspapers, in my opinion, need definite action should be taken to point out there are factual areas as well as serious consequences flowing from distorted and factually incorrect newspaper articles dated August 9, 1943.

Index

A

B

P

Q

R

T

Tabernacle Baptist Church, 143
"Talented Tenth", 11, 16
Tallahatchie River, 126
Taylor, Norman "Kansas", 74-77, 82
"That Old Gang of Mine", 31
Thatcher, Harold W., 16
Third IL. District, 109
Third Ward, 19
Thomas, Clarence, 179
Thoreau, Henry, 105
Till, Emmett Louis, 126
Tizol, Juan, 88
Topeka, Kansas, 123
Towns, Clarence, 109
Townsend, Willard, 118
Travis, Dempsey, 1-12, 19, 20, 24, 28, 30, 33, 35, 44, 53, 64-67, 89, 91, 106, 122, 130, 132-
    134, 139, 142, 144, 148, 152, 153, 156, 157, 159, 160, 162, 167, 171
Travis, Louis, 23, 30, 33, 39, 48, 49, 59, 64
Travis, Mittie, 4, 20, 22, 23, 33, 64, 57-60
Travis, Moselynne (see also Moselynne Hardwick), 9, 111, 113
Travis Insurance Co., 146
Travis Realty Co. , 145, 151
Truman, Harry S. , 95, 124
Trumbull Park, 109
Turner, Milton, 59
Tuskegee Airman, 118

U

Union Station, Washington, D.C., 87
Union Stockyard, 50, 102, 103, 110
United Mortgage Bankers of America, Inc. (UMBA), 58, 81, 99, 152, 153, 155-157, 161
United Packinghouse Workers of America (C.I.O.), 110
United States Armed Forces, 58, 81, 99, 124
U.S. Attorney General, 153
U. S. Claims Court, New York, N.Y., 132
U.S. Department of Housing, 152
United States Supreme Court , 122, 123, 137, 150
Universal Savings and Loan, 116
University of Chicago, 11
U.S.O., 65
USS Arizona, 56

V

V.E. Day, (Victory in Europe), 95
Veteran's Administration (VA), 107, 150, 153
View Park, Calif, 117
"Violets Blue", 32
Voluntary Home Mortgage Credit Program (VHMCP), 151

W

Y